The Art of American Book Covers
1875-1930

1. [Unknown], 1881. *Mr. Bodley Abroad* by Horace E. Scudder.
Boston: Houghton, Mifflin and Company. 21.3 x 17.5

Printed paper wrapped over boards and spine cloth. The artist
who created this is still unknown, but had skills similar to those
of painter/illustrator John La Farge. This design anticipates
Constructivist, Futurist, and Abstract Expressionist paradigms, as
well as the influence of Japanese asymmetry (see also p. 82).

THE ART OF
AMERICAN BOOK COVERS
1875-1930

by

Richard Minsky

NEW YORK

GEORGE BRAZILLER, INC.

2010

Published in the United States of America by George Braziller, Inc., New York.
Copyright © 2010 George Braziller, Inc.
Text and images © 2010 Richard Minsky

For information, please address the publisher:

George Braziller, Inc.
171 Madison Avenue
New York, New York 10016

Library of Congress Cataloging-in-Publication Data

Minsky, Richard.
    The art of American book covers : 1875-1930 / by Richard Minsky.
        p. cm.
    Includes bibliographical references.
    ISBN 978-0-8076-1602-4 (alk. paper)
    1. Book covers--United States--History--19th century. 2. Book covers--United States--History--20th century. I. Title.

    NC973.5.U6M56 2010
    741.6'40973--dc22

                                            2009051488
Design © 2010 Richard Minsky
Printed and bound by Asia Pacific Offset (China).

First Edition

To Barbara and Samantha

Acknowledgements

I am grateful to have a small group of advisors who engage in e-mail discussions of design and attribution. Without their collective wisdom, which adds up to over 150 years of studying and collecting publishers' bindings, this book would not be nearly as extensive, beautiful, and informative.

Sue Allen was my first inspiration. In 1976 her book, *Victorian Bookbindings*, made me aware of commercial book covers as an area of serious research. It was published by The University of Chicago Press and included three color microfiche containing photographs of 251 bindings. While preparing the materials for this book and my two previous volumes on *American Decorated Publishers' Bindings*, I have called on Sue many times, and she has generously shared her wealth of knowledge.

In 2000 The Grolier Club hosted an exhibition, The Art of Publishers' Bookbindings 1815-1915, curated by Ellen K. Morris and Edward Levin, who produced an extraordinary catalog. Ellen and Edward have been of immense help, showing me pristine examples of many books in their home, discussing the antecedents of the designs and reading drafts of my texts.

Marty Barringer, retired Special Collections Librarian at Georgetown University, has, together with his wife Penelope, built up a large private collection in this field. His bibliographic expertise and knowledge of design history were invaluable, particularly for his corrections to the Introduction.

Stuart Walker, Conservator at the Boston Public Library, is exceptionally knowledgeable of this field, particularly of Sarah Wyman Whitman. He has helped with attributions, suggested books, and identified sources of biographical information.

Over a thousand e-mails have been exchanged with John Lehner, who has advised me on everything from the intricacies of various artists' lettering styles to the publishers each artist worked for in a particular year. John is a contagiously obsessive collector, and sends me images of book covers almost every day. He has been acquiring publishers' bindings of this period since the 1960s. This year we met in person for the first time, when I visited him in California and spent two days looking at his books. He graciously scanned several of them for inclusion here, and he gets picture credit for 58, 76, 93, 125, and 140. John's wife Marlene gets credit for cooking a fabulous Greek dinner.

I was never a good typist, so reading this book will be less of a hardship thanks to the keen eye of copy editor Maria A. Dering, who caught a plethora of errors and straightened out stylistic inconsistencies. But don't blame her for the variations in publishers' names that occur throughout the text and captions. She advised me of the standardized forms, but I take responsibility for leaving them as they are. For the most part, this is how they appear on the title page of each book. In some cases this varied from one edition to the next, and the cover art that is shown here may not be on a different edition, or even a different printing of the same edition.

The layout and design of this book were assisted by the staff at George Braziller, Inc. Maxwell Heller and Andrea Rollefson reviewed many drafts and provided detailed feedback as the book took shape.

The people who really made this book possible are Barbara Slate and Samantha, who put up with my disappearing into the studio to write it and only have seen me at breakfast and dinner for months. Their love and encouragement keep me going.

There are likely to be more errors found after publication, and I am responsible for them. If you discover any, please send a note so corrections can be made in the event of a reprinting.

Richard Minsky
Stockport, NY
November, 2009

Introduction

In the 1870s book cover art in the United States entered a Golden Age that lasted more than fifty years. Some of the work is startling for its prescience and can be associated with art movements that occurred decades after the books were produced.

Publishers commissioned contemporary painters, architects, and stained glass designers to create covers that would grab the eye of bookstore browsers. Artists experimented with new visual concepts and production processes in an era of rapid technological, social, and aesthetic evolution. These artists were in the forefront not only of book cover design, but of visual culture. In the following pages you will see works by early precursors to Malevich, Marinetti, Kandinsky, Kline, Escher, and other artists. One wonders if the artists had these books in their childhood homes.

Identifying the cover artists helped publishers to sell books. Houghton, Mifflin took the lead in America in 1887, featuring Mrs. Henry Whitman's name as the cover designer in their advertising, but showed no images of the covers. Sarah Wyman Whitman created hundreds of covers for Houghton and influenced many other artists. In the decade that followed, other publishers' advertisements and catalogs featured cover artists such as Frank Hazenplug, Will Bradley, and Bruce Rogers, who had become so well known that their names appeared without pictures of the covers.

As early as the 1840s, Americans were buying books as decorative objects for their homes as well as works of literature. This was not the same as buying sets of books by the yard to decorate the shelves of

Aboard the Mavis, Dodd, Mead and Co., 1880.

a home library. The beautiful covers of individual books were meant to be seen, not hidden on shelves with only their spines exposed.

By 1894, American artists' monograms or devices regularly appeared on book covers. These took various forms: Sarah Whitman used a flaming heart with her initials; W. W. Denslow was known by his stylized sea horse; Earl Stetson Crawford by a crowned "C." At the beginning of the twentieth century, more than 200 monograms or devices were in use.

Books are pervasive cultural objects, and for many years the artwork on them was taken for granted. The study of book cover art is a relatively new field, having begun only in the 1960s with the work of Charles Gullans and John Espey at UCLA, followed by the independent scholar Sue Allen in the mid-1970s. For three decades Sue has been promoting interest in this field, and her courses at Rare Book School (an independent non-profit educational institute based at the University of Virginia) have educated and inspired a generation of curators, librarians, and collectors.

Some of the most exciting designs are as yet unattributed. One of the great designs of this period is the wraparound cover on Richard Markham's 1880 *Aboard the Mavis*, published by Dodd, Mead. The same artist was responsible for a Houghton,

Monograms on covers by Margaret Armstrong, Sarah Wyman Whitman, Earl Stetson Crawford, and William Wallace Denslow.

Mifflin series featuring the adventures of the Bodley family, represented here by *Mr. Bodley Abroad* [1, frontispiece]. A work such as this, with a masterful sense of composition, classical drawing technique, and exhibiting a vision decades ahead of its time, required an artist with the skills and sensibility of John La Farge. Although there is no evidence that La Farge designed any book covers, we do know that he worked as an illustrator for Houghton, Scribner, and other publishers. He knew and taught several of the younger cover artists, which gives rise to the enticing speculation that La Farge was either involved with, or created, book cover art.

The British Influence

Several American publishers maintained offices in London. This group included Harper, Macmillan,

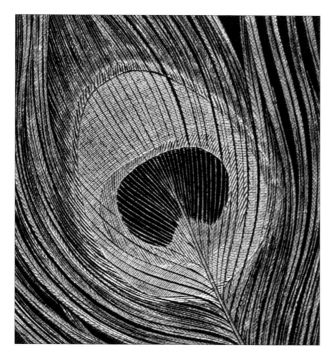

Detail from *The New Day*, 1876 [2]. This peacock feather design achieves luminance by hand engraving the lines at different angles, and cross-hatching with different textures. Stamped in fine gold leaf, it is as beautiful and satisfying to look at as a master's brushwork on canvas.

Century, Funk & Wagnalls and Putnam in New York; Lippincott in Philadelphia; Luce, Ginn, and Lamson-Wolffe in Boston; and Revell in Chicago. D. Appleton had been importing British books since the 1840s. By the 1860s Cassell and Routledge had branches in the United States. By the 1880s, London publishers Longman's, Hodder & Stoughton and John Lane had offices in New York. Artistic and literary ideas flowed quickly across the Atlantic on steamships that took less than a week to make the crossing.

British book cover art in the last third of the nineteenth century was influenced by two distinct artistic trends—the Arts and Crafts Movement, associated with John Ruskin, William Morris, and T. J. Cobden-Sanderson, and the Aesthetic Movement, associated with Dante Gabriel Rossetti and industrial designer and ornamentalist Christopher Dresser. The latter's modernist methodology was codified in several books, particularly *Principles of Decorative Design* (four 1870 articles printed as a book in 1873), and *Studies in Design* (1874). American cover artists would have been familiar with the works of Dresser, who lectured in Philadelphia at the Pennsylvania Museum and School of Industrial Art in 1876.

Charles Eastlake's popular book *Hints on Household Taste in Furniture, Upholstery, and Other Details* was published in England in 1868, and in the USA in 1872. Many book covers were produced that capitalized on the popularity of the "Eastlake style" (see p. 23). Although it was considered "modern" at the time, today it looks more like a vestige of the Victorian era than a precursor to Modernism.

The transition to new visual paradigms produced remarkable effects when combined with the highly evolved skills of traditional die-engravers. This is seen in the gold peacock feather on the 1876 cover of Richard Gilder's poems, *The New Day*, published in New York by Scribner, Armstrong and Company [2]. The extremely fine detailing makes the image shimmer, with even slight movements causing one part or another of the cover to flash more brightly.

The die work creates the illusion of dimensionality with flat gold stamping that one wants to touch to see if it is embossed.

The peacock feather was a favorite device of the Aesthetic Movement. This book was published the same year that James McNeill Whistler, a friend of Gilder, created his famous Peacock Room for the London home of Frederick R. Leyland.

One of the most important steps in the development of American cover art came in 1878, on Bayard Taylor's *Prince Deukalion: A Lyrical Drama* [3]. This edition, issued in Boston by Houghton, Osgood, had a cover that was neither new nor by an American artist. It was created by Rossetti for Algernon Swinburne's *Atalanta in Calydon*, published in London by Edward Moxon and Co. in 1865. Taylor knew Swinburne, and also was a friend of Samuel Bancroft, Jr., who owned Bancroft Mills in Wilmington, Delaware. That firm manufactured the faux vellum cloth for the cover of this book.

Would an author be so involved in a book's production as to select the cover art and the cloth? Taylor was apprenticed to a printer early in his career, but became a poet, novelist, and popular travel writer. This led to his appointment as United States Minister to Germany in 1878 while *Prince Deukalion* was being produced. Shortly after arriving in Berlin he began suffering with a digestive disorder. *Deukalion* was published in November, and he held a copy in his

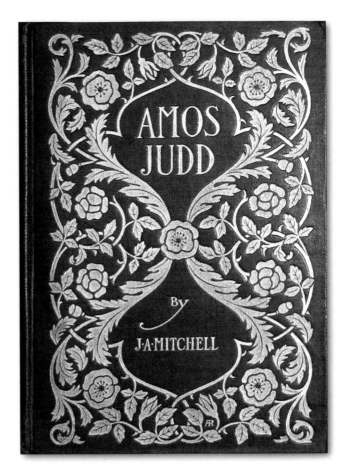

Scribner's 1901 edition of *Amos Judd* featured a cover by Amy Richards that was stongly influenced by the British Arts and Crafts Movement, particularly the work of T. J. Cobden-Sanderson.

hands just a few weeks before his death at age 53.

The Rossetti design, with its adaptation of Japanese emblems, was then an anomaly in American publishing. What made it important was its influence on a young artist who began designing book covers a few years later.

Sarah Wyman Whitman was a gifted painter as well as a prominent Boston hostess, married to a prosperous wool merchant. She was a student of the painter William Morris Hunt, and had studied in France with Hunt's teacher, Thomas Couture. She apprenticed herself to John La Farge, who, among his

Detail of Rossetti's 1865 design, left, used by Houghton on the 1878 edition of *Prince Deukalion*. To the right is a detail from Sarah Whitman's 1880 cover on the *Verses* of Susan Coolidge.

many artistic skills, was a master at stained glass. He resurrected medieval techniques and developed new methods and materials. La Farge had also studied with Couture and Hunt. Hunt, during his period in France, studied with Jean-François Millet, and brought the influence of the Barbizon School to La Farge and Whitman. After her apprenticeship with La Farge, Sarah Whitman opened her own stained glass studio and was highly sought after for commissions.

The earliest example of Whitman's book cover design is the *Verses* by Susan Coolidge (Roberts Brothers, 1880) [4], for which she adapted Rossetti's stylized Japanese medallions.

The public responded well to her work, and by 1884 Houghton commissioned Whitman regularly. Her lettering and composition were emulated and imitated by many others, including New York artist Alice Cordelia Morse [6].

Women and Cover Art

Book cover design was one of the few professions that welcomed women. Perhaps this was because women were a large part of the book market, and a cover informed by a feminine sensibility might sell more books. Women artists certainly did change the look of book covers, and also provided themselves with a source of income.

Alice Cordelia Morse, who studied painting and stained glass with John La Farge in New York, became a prominent creator of cover art. Her work spanned a wide variety of styles, and was influenced by historical bookbindings. Mindell Dubansky, librarian and book conservator at the Metropolitan Museum of Art, discovered a box of sample Morse covers some years ago and has spent a decade researching her life and work, culminating in an exhibition at the Grolier Club and a monograph.[1]

Alice Morse organized an exhibition of women illustrators and book cover designers for the Woman's

Building in the World's Columbian Exposition in Chicago in 1893. She also wrote the chapters on illustrators and binding designers for the Exposition's *Art and Handicraft in the Woman's Building*, and the ornate cover design is attributed to her [7].

Orientalism

During the last third of the nineteenth century all things Oriental were in vogue, especially in art. Arabic, Moorish, and Indian geometric patterns were adapted to book covers, and artists developed new styles based on the asymmetry of Japanese design. Several reference books on Oriental art and design

Edwin Austin Abbey, 1881. *The Land of the Midnight Sun.* A new starting date for Art Nouveau?

---

1 See Dubansky in the bibliography, p. 132.

were published in Britain and the United States, beginning with Owen Jones' classic *The Grammar of Ornament* in 1856. [2]

Two Alice Morse tours-de-force of Moorish and Arabesque design were created for Putnam's editions of Washington Irving's *The Alhambra*, 1891 [9] and *Conquest of Granada*, 1893 [10].

Japanese color woodcuts, *ukiyo-e*, were all the rage, particularly in France, in the 1860s and '70s. "Japonisme," as Jules Claretie dubbed it in 1872, affected book cover design as it did all the other arts. Hokusai's *Thirty-six Views of Mount Fuji*, Hiroshige's *The Fifty-three Stations of the Tokaido*, and similar series had a powerful influence on book cover artists.. Thomas Buford Meteyard's 1894 cover for Stevenson's *The Ebb Tide* for Stone & Kimball is an asymmetrical seascape done in line, clearly influenced by the Japanese [11]. The anonymous 1898 cover on *Love and Rocks* uses a similar compositional framework [12].

Art Nouveau

The Aesthetic Movement developed from the interaction of Orientalist features with Western aesthetics, and that current continued into the decades that followed. British architect Arthur Mackmurdo's cover for his book *Wren's City Churches* (London, 1883) is often cited as the first example of Art Nouveau. It is surprising that the earlier covers created by Pennsylvania-born artist Edwin Austin Abbey for Harper & Brothers are not mentioned in the history of this movement.

Abbey's work was prototypical of Art Nouveau, and likely known to Mackmurdo. Abbey moved to England in 1878 and became prominent on the British art scene. The 1881 edition of du Chaillou's *The Land of the Midnight Sun* (p. 12) and *Selections from the Poetry of Robert Herrick*, 1882 [19] employ similar motifs, with the latter incorporating the title

Will Bradley, 1894. *In Russet and Silver* by Edmund Gosse. Stone and Kimball, Chicago [21].

in the cover design. Abbey continued the evolution of his organic style with the lettering taking a bold, dominant place in *Sketching Rambles in Holland*, 1885 [20].

American cover artists incorporated elements of Art Nouveau into many designs for the next two decades. Examples in the current selection include Frederick W. Gookin's 1893 cover for *Favorite Dishes* [120], Elihu Vedder's 1894 *Rubaiyat* [88], and Margaret Armstrong's 1901 *Candle-Lightin' Time* [66]

The Picture Plane

In 1894 Will Bradley was commissioned by the Chicago publisher Herbert Stone to create a cover for *In Russet and Silver* [21], a book of poetry by Edmund Gosse. The forest and mountains appear to be continuous from the front cover across the spine to the back cover, but in fact the front and back cover images are identical, with the spine treatment bridging the left and right edges of the picture. The landscape is reduced to abstract silhouettes, yet retains a naturalistic feeling. The trees are the color of the cloth, so only two colors of stamping were needed to produce the covers..

The foreground trees in the cloth color rest on the picture plane, with two planes, the mountains and the sky, apparently receding behind it. Prior to this, the illusion of pictorial depth was created by perspective drawing. Here, Bradley's use of color in flat planes to create depth of field was a significant change in concept. The title plane floats in front of the image, but since it is the same silver as the back plane, it creates a tension, with the same metallic color simultaneously advancing and receding. The title is stamped into the cloth surface, physically penetrating the picture plane, creating the paradox of being both optically in front of, and physically behind, the trees.

Many artists were influenced by Bradley, and furthered his concepts by adding elements that moved the image through the planes or added layers and figures to create different illusions of depth and pictorial space [22, 30, and 70].

The Decorative Designers

Many individual artists are included in this book, but the most prolific creator of book cover art was The Decorative Designers (DD), a small company that operated from 1895 to 1932.

The firm was founded by Henry Thayer, who hired Emma Redington Lee to work with him. They married in 1909, and she changed her name to Lee Thayer. Several important artists worked for DD at various times, including Rome K. Richardson, Charles Buckles Falls, and Jay Chambers. Many designs were group efforts, with appropriate division of labor. Henry, an architect, was a master at lettering. Jay did much of the figurative illustration. Lee excelled at decorative borders, but also had an impeccable sense of composition and created some of the company's finest covers.

Team effort at DD was particularly effective on works that combined the best attributes of each artist. *The Holy Land*, commissioned by Century in 1910, has it all—an ornate border, a pictorial scene, and fine lettering [75].

Lee was responsible for the scintillating repeat pattern of irises in bright and matte textured gold on *The Epic of Hades* [46] and the exquisite cover on Hearn's *Shadowings* [13]. Her stylistic range is formidable, as with other masters of this era. Economic considerations were partly responsible: books were designed and produced for specific markets. There were different tastes to satisfy. Additionally, covers often reflected the content of the books. Lee emerged

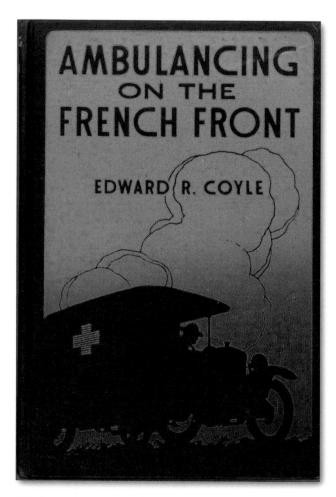

This dramatic 1918 cover from the Britton Publishing Company in New York was produced in one stamping with a split fountain. The ink reservoir was divided with turquoise on one side and orange on the other. 19.3 x 13

from the Victorian sensibility of the previous generation and adopted new stylistic influences, including Japanese woodcuts, as in *The Song of the Wave*, 1898 [93], which also uses textured gold brilliantly. Bright and matte gold were created by texturing different areas on the stamping die, so that one impression would create a variety of gold effects. A classic example is her 1899 repeating pattern for *Nature Studies in Berkshire* [92], which combines textured gold with elements of Art Nouveau and Arts and Crafts.

Artists across the country kept up with each other's published work, and were influenced by it. This makes it harder for us to be sure of attributions on many unsigned cover designs. *The First Violin*, published by Brentano's in 1899 [45], has lettering with stylistic details used by Henry Thayer, and the use of bright and matte gold with a repeat thistle pattern is much like the work of Lee Thayer. Only the lack of the familiar DD logo, or any other attribution within the book, prevents this exceptional cover from being assigned to DD with certainty.

Charles Gullans and John Espey, pioneers in the study of American publishers' bindings, conducted two interviews with Lee Thayer in May and July of 1970, and organized a DD exhibition at UCLA in October of that year, with an essay and checklist to accompany it.

The Split Fountain

One technique that the DD firm used to great advantage is the *split fountain* or *fountain blend*. It refers to the ink fountain on a printing press. By placing dividers in the fountain and filling it with different inks, it is possible to print two or more colors on one die (the engraved metal plate with the image). The rollers that transfer the ink from the fountain to the die blend the colors where they meet. Other designers used the technique occasionally, but most of the American split fountain productions were created by The Decorative Designers.

The use of this technique in the United States was facilitated by the Colt's Armory Press, engineered by John Thompson and based on the "Universal" press of Merritt Gally. Colt's produced this powerful platen press from 1873 to 1902, the year that Thompson bought the patent rights from them. Generally regarded as the best hand-fed presses ever built, they could use either ink or a heated platen for embossing, and produced enough pressure to stamp a cloth book cover. The presses were manufactured by the Thompson-National Press Co. into the 1980s.

Ambulancing on the French Front (Britton, 1918) is an unsigned cover that looks like the work of Jay Chambers, who worked for DD (p. 14). It demonstrates what can be achieved with a single impression and one stamping die. The wartime economy and rationing limited the number of gold-stamped and multiple-die covers that publishers could produce.

Thomas Watson Ball

The covers of T. W. Ball were completely neglected by scholars of binding design for many years. Gullans and Espey did not mention him in their 1979 essay in *Collectible Books*, despite listing "The Major Designers" and "Other Noteworthy Designers." Ball worked in several distinct styles and rarely monogrammed his work.

Fortunately, Ball compiled a portfolio with some of his binding designs, likely for the purpose of showing these to publishers. His portfolio was acquired by the collector Robert Metzdorf, who loaned it to Sue Allen in 1972 for an exhibition she organized in Chicago. The portfolio passed from Metzdorf's estate to the University of Rochester in 1975. Only the front covers are in it, with no spines or indication of publisher or date. Acquiring copies of the actual books to photograph was a challenge.

Ball often painted in the Pointillist and Impressionist styles. He made many nautical paintings; his fascination with ships and the sea influenced his cover art. *The Merry Anne* (1904) uses decoratively textured fields to create the feeling of the water's surface by translating the impressionist technique of his painting to the medium of die-stamped cloth.

Fortune's Boats [31], done for Houghton in 1900, features a gorgeous combination of gold and silver with stylized silhouettes.

A combination of Ball's styles appears in a series of designs for Houghton beginning in 1901 with *In The Levant* [35]. That cover is in his portfolio, and on pages 52-53 are two other covers with similar use of silhouetted buildings on a gold background. Each design features different Ball elements.

Silhouettes

Thomas Watson Ball was a master of creating covers that used silhouettes, either for the complete design or for particular elements of it. His 1900 design for *Lords of the North* by A. C. Laut [33] is particularly

Thomas Watson Ball. Detail from *Lords of the North* by A. C. Laut [33].

interesting because there is a reflection of the silhouette in the water. The smooth ripples from the motion of the canoe and the smaller ripples further out tell us about the speed of the canoe and the breeze. The angle and length of the shadows suggest the position of the sun. In several other designs Ball sets the silhouette against a striated sky, patterned water, or both.

In *Visiting the Sin* [32] and *Harper's Pictorial History of the War with Spain* [34], Ball creates compelling and evocative images with silhouettes in a flattened pictorial space.

The outline of an object is all we usually need to identify it. With a simplified image that eliminates color, shading, and interior detail, the mind not only recognizes the pattern quickly, but often our imagination inserts missing elements.

Studies in perceptual physiology suggest that there may be an additional factor that makes these images enjoyable. The chemistry of cognition rewards the pleasure center of the brain when a pattern is identified, as when solving a puzzle.

Many cover artists used silhouettes for the complete design or as counterpoint to a detailed background. The effective but unsigned 1899 design on *Two Women in the Klondike* [38] employs another artistic tool, the partial figure. In the same way that the mind fills in the silhouette details, it completes the image of a woman seen from behind, which in this case merges into the cloth left, right, and bottom.

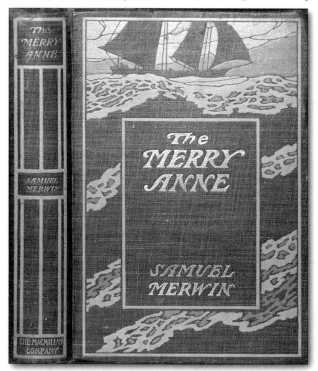

Thomas Watson Ball. *The Merry Anne* by Samuel Merwin. Illustrations and decorations by Thomas Fogarty. New York & London: The Macmillan Company, 1904. 19.7 x 13.6

Another approach using one color and gold is employed to create the vibrant design by Edward S. Holloway on *At the Time Appointed* [72]. The stark and simple dark green trees on red cloth create the sensation of looking up, with a disturbing feeling akin to vertigo. Floating the gold title in front of the image helps the illusion. It is a superb use of color. The gold advances in front of the picture plane and the green recedes. The red cloth advances on the green. Having the background advance on the foreground creates perceptual confusion and spatial disorientation, which contribute to the effect.

A publisher's budget for binding production was a significant factor, and artists were told how many colors they could use in a particular cover design. By using the cloth color as a pictorial element, artists added a color to their palette.

In binding design white is a color, and the unidentified artist of the 1904 cover for *The Lure O' Gold* [98] hinted at the angle of the sun by having a few lines intrude into the silhouette on the port side of the ship's hull. There is a slight ripple on the sea, evoked by a simple extension of light from the white sky to define the water.

Symmetrical and Repeating Patterns

Throughout the history of bookbinding design, symmetry and pattern repetition have given a sense of security and equilibrium to the covers. This period was no exception, and there are some striking examples. The motifs span Oriental [9], floral [59], Art Nouveau [41], Arts and Crafts [47], and Neoclassical [49] styles.

Marion L. Peabody

Marion L. Peabody was a master of cover design who incorporated Art Nouveau, Arts and Crafts, and prototypical Social Realism into her work. *Love Triumphant* (1906) uses a shaped embossing die to create three-dimensional apples on a flat tree. *The Fleeing Nymph* (1905) [90], in three tones of

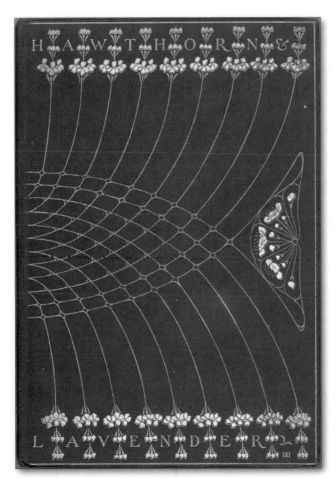

Vertical Symmetry and horizontal asymmetry: Henry Thayer, 1901. *Hawthorn and Lavender by* William Ernest Henley. New York and London: Harper and Brothers. 19.7 x 13

Marion L. Peabody, 1906. Detail from *Love Triumphant* by Frederic Lawrence Knowles. Boston: Dana Estes & Company 18.6 x 12.4

textured gold, features a nude figure in keeping with the subject matter.

Peabody created covers for all the major Boston publishers and also worked as an illustrator, most notably for Richard G. Badger. Most of her bindings are signed MP or MLP, though the monogram is done differently on each.

In 1899 she produced a spectacular double cover design for *The Loom of Destiny* [89], a tribute to what can be done in a single stamping of white metal on black cloth.

The Up Grade [91] was published by Little, Brown in 1910. It uses a strong arm and hand image, combined with leaf forms and swirling vinelike leaf and frond organic shapes. Peabody's figurative style anticipates Social Realism of the 1930s.

Margaret Armstrong

The best known and most widely collected cover artist is Margaret Armstrong. Gullans and Espey catalogued 314 of her covers in 1991.[3]

Born in 1867 to a New York family at the heart of the social and cultural elite, her circle included

Margaret Armstrong, 1900. Detail from *Pippa Passes* [58].

artists John La Farge, William Merritt Chase, Stanford White, and Winslow Homer. Margaret's father, David Maitland Armstrong, was a painter, stained glass artist, and diplomat.

She sold her first binding design in 1890 to the Chicago publisher A. C. McClurg. Despite the popu-

larity of Sarah Whitman's covers for Houghton, it was still difficult for women to break into the field. Armstrong sent out examples of her work using her initials and surname: M. N. Armstrong. She rose quickly to prominence, and by 1891 was designing covers for Scribner's and Harper. Her work was included in the important 1894 Grolier Club exhibition *Commercial Bookbindings*.

Armstrong's work benefited from mastery of symmetrical pattern, a painterly eye for color, and the effective use of bright and textured gold. All the major publishers commissioned covers from her and spent the money required to produce high quality

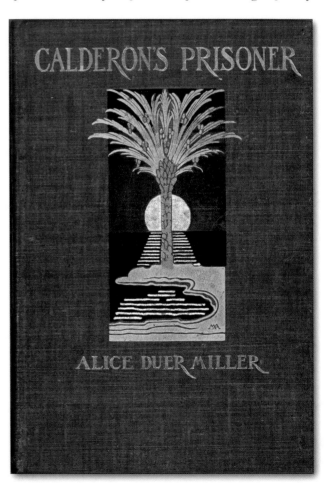

Margaret Armstrong, 1903. *Calderon's Prisoner* by Alice Duer Miller. New York: Charles Scribner's Sons. 19.6 x 13.6

3. *Margaret Armstrong and American Trade Bindings* (see p. 132).

bindings stamped with several impressions in color and gold. Her artwork sold enough books to warrant the investment.

For her part, she was willing to produce multiple versions of the artwork so that the engravers could make several variant editions of her most elaborate designs. Some were issued in different colors or complexities of stamping to suit different tastes and purses.

Frank Hazenplug

One of the most prolific cover artists was Frank Hazenplug, who changed his name to Hazen in 1911. He began doing book covers at the age of twenty in Chicago for Stone & Kimball in 1894, became their house designer, and was responsible for covers on the majority of their books.

When Stone's output decreased, Hazenplug produced work for the other Chicago and Indianapolis publishers. In 1908 George Doran, vice-president of the Chicago publishing house Fleming Revell, moved to New York to start his own company and Hazenplug did many of their covers. Three years later Hazenplug followed Doran to New York.

Overall, Hazenplug's work varied widely, from simple, elegantly lettered covers to highly formal patterns as well as figures and landscapes. Among

Frank Hazenplug, 1913. *The Woods* by Douglas Malloch. Chicago: American Lumberman; New York: George H. Doran Company, n.d., 1913. Olive green cloth stamped in white and blue~gray treescape. In gray paper dust jacket with the same design in dark green and blue. 20.4 x 13.9

his greatest achievements was the 1896 stylized artichoke design on Richard Le Galliene's *Prose Fancies* [41].

His exploration of the use of trees as a motif built upon Will Bradley's 1896 design on *In Russet and Silver* (p. 13). A relatively simple example is Hazenplug's 1913 cover for Doran on *The Woods* by Douglas Malloch. A second plane of tree silhouettes is stamped in blue~gray "behind" the trees in the cloth color. The background plane is stamped in white, creating the illusion that light is filtering through a forest.

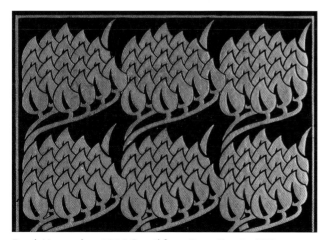

Frank Hazenplug, 1896. Detail from *Prose Fancies* [41].

Also in 1913, Hazenplug took this concept to another level on Kipling's *The Jungle Book* [30], published by The Century Company. He added a third plane of trees, a gold background, and foreground silhouette figures. This binding also features a fully stamped spine pictorial in the same color combination.

Blanche McManus Mansfield

Born in Louisiana in 1870, Blanche McManus studied art in London and Paris before opening her Chicago

Blanche McManus Mansfield , 1897. *Blown Away* by Richard Mansfield. Boston: L. C. Page and Company. At first glance the covers appear mirrored, but a close look shows the mountain edges and buildings are different. 19.3 x 13.3

Blanche McManus Mansfield , 1897. *A Charm of Birds* by Rose Porter. New York: E. R. Herrick & Company. Also issued in green cloth. 19.5 x 11.8

studio in 1893. In 1896 she was doing covers for Stone & Kimball in Chicago and Dodd, Mead in New York. Her first children's book, *The True Mother Goose*, was published by Lamson, Wolffe in Boston the same year.

McManus' 1897 cover for *A Charm of Birds* uses curved gold lines to add movement to a scene that otherwise might appear flat and lifeless. She used similar swirling lines that year for L. C. Page on Richard Mansfield's *Blown Away*, a striking and fanciful double-cover pictorial with symmetrical nearly identical images connected by a spine panel.

Blanche married Francis Miltoun Mansfield in 1898. They traveled through Europe and North Africa, creating illustrated travel books together that were published by Page from 1903 to 1912. For these books he used the name Francis Miltoun.

Who's Who in America for 1910 shows Blanche Mansfield's studio address as Martigues, France. Francis then became the United States Consular Agent in Toulon, where Blanche finished her illustrated book *The American Woman Abroad*, published by Dodd, Mead in 1911.

No work of Blanche McManus Mansfield has surfaced that is documented as later than 1912. The monogram on *Utah : The Land of Blossoming Valleys* by George Wharton James (Page, 1922) is monogrammed M c M [81]. Stylistically it is similar to a design done in 1899 by T. W. Ball [79], and another unsigned design from 1900 [80]. Page might have had this design on file.

Her life after 1912 is shrouded in mystery, with one report suggesting she was confined to a mental institution in New Orleans from the 1920s until her death in 1935.

Poster Format

The use of flat color brought the spatial, narrative and figurative qualities of the lithographed poster onto the stamped book cover. The influence of French Art Nouveau posters is seen in Adolphe Borie's 1896 artwork for *Chap-book Stories.*

Dust jackets have come with books since the earliest days of publishers' bindings. The poster format naturally migrated to the dust jacket. Some books, like *Little Injun* (1927), used the same image on the dust jacket and the book cover. Eventually the publishers abandoned the stamped cover as an unnecessary marketing expense, and the dust jacket took over the role of visually selling the book.

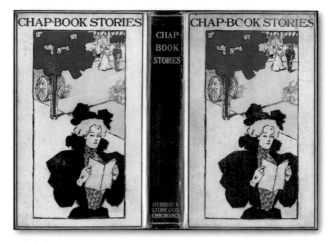

Adolphe E. Borie, lettering by Claude Bragdon , 1896. *Chap-book Stories*. Chicago: Herbert S. Stone & Co. Cream cloth stamped in blue, black, yellow, and green. The attribution to Borie, then an art student in Pennsylvania, is by Sidney Kramer. Others assign it to Will Bradley. 17.7 x 11.2

The original role of the dust jacket was sacrificial—to protect the cover from the elements. This one absorbed the grime and wear of handling, preserving the cover art beautifully.

The Decorative Designers, 1927. *Little Injun* by Lowell Otus Reese. New York: Thomas Y. Crowell Company. Black and yellow on orange cloth. 19.5 x 13.5

Variants

It can be difficult to determine whether a particular copy of a book represents the artist's intention or results from a decision by the publisher.

Many covers were used on subsequent printings of a book with some element changed. Even if it is the same printing of an edition, the binding cloth may be buckram on one copy and linen weave or pebble grain on another. The cloth color may be different. The stamping colors may change. One copy of a book may have the cover four colors and gold, while another with the same design will be in two colors with no gold.

Some artists, like Margaret Armstrong, produced variants of the design as part of their commission [see 62 and 63]. Many times, however, the change was a cost-cutting decision, or represented a way to distinguish between printings or editions of a text. In some cases, the printing plates and stamping dies were acquired by a different publisher. Changes were often made without the approval of the artist.

(Unknown), 1880. *An Involuntary Voyage* by Lucien Biart. Translated by Mrs. Cashel Hoey and John Lillie. New York: Harper & Brothers. Blue cloth on beveled boards stamped with gold mast, title in maroon and gold pennant. A second copy in green cloth, otherwise identical. 19.8 x 13.

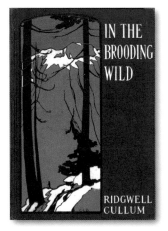

Charles Livingston Bull, 1905. *In the Brooding Wild* by Ridgwell Cullum. Boston: L. C. Page & Company. Blue cloth stamped in black, white, orange and gray winter treescape with skier and mountains, white title on cover and spine. 19.7 x 13.5. Right is a 1909 reprint with a variant of this design from A. L. Burt Company. Gray~green cloth stamped in black, yellow and light gray, yellow title on cover and spine. 19.3 x 12.8

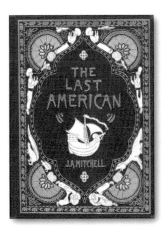

Albert D. Blashfield. , 1902. *The Last American* by J. A. Mitchell. New York: Frederick A. Stoles Company. Blue cloth stamped in red, white, yellow, and gold with a Persian motif, animals and cartoonish characters being bitten on the nose by mosquitoes, a ship in the center, gold title on cover and spine. The variant is apparently identical within, but the stamping has pink instead of white. 19.6 x 14.4

Art for Commerce

Prior to publication a salesman would take sample books door-to-door, showing part of the text and illustrations, a stamped cover, and a choice of binding styles, often in cloth and leather. The customers could order from the comfort of their homes and receive the book that fit their taste, decor, and budget.

In the back of many sample books were ruled pages to record the orders. Thousands of examples survive, many with the subscribers' names and preferences, serving as an archival record of tastes and artistic trends.

The modern designs exemplified in the current selection are rarely seen in these presentations. They constitute a small percentage of the bindings produced, and the "boutique" audience for these designs may not have been the target market of door-to-door solicitation.

The End

By 1910 the pictorial dust jacket had largely replaced the expensive stamping of cloth covers [117]. Printed paper onlays were also glued directly to the cloth in lieu of part or all of the stamping [119]. The production of commercial bindings as exquisite decorative objects declined rapidly, and during World War I, was exacerbated by rationing and the economy. The boom decade after the war enabled a resurgence in demand for stamped covers, but the Stock Market Crash of 1929 and the Great Depression made the extra expense untenable. And so ended the golden age of commercial bookbindings.

Note: all the dimensions for book covers are given in centimeters.

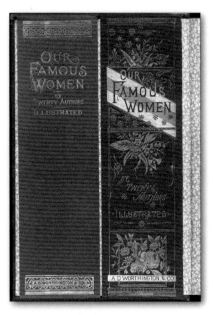

1883 Salesman's sample book for *Our Famous Women*. Hartford: A. D. Worthington & Co. Victorian eclectic excess was still popular, but the inside covers also showed a simpler cloth binding and two styles in leather at different price points. The cover design uses Eastlake style ornaments. 23 x 15.2

2. [Unknown*], 1876 . *The New Day: A poem in Songs and Sonnets* by Richard Watson Gilder. Illustrations engraved by Henry Marsh. New York: Scribner, Armstrong and Company. 17.8 x 13.5

Gold-stamped peacock feather on blue cloth over beveled boards. A brilliant example of the engraver's art—both in the quality of technique used to execute it and the illumination that emanates from the image.

* This cover is often attributed to the author's wife Helena, whose drawings, which include peacock feathers, were engraved to illustrate this volume, but there is no evidence that she chose the bold diagonal format.

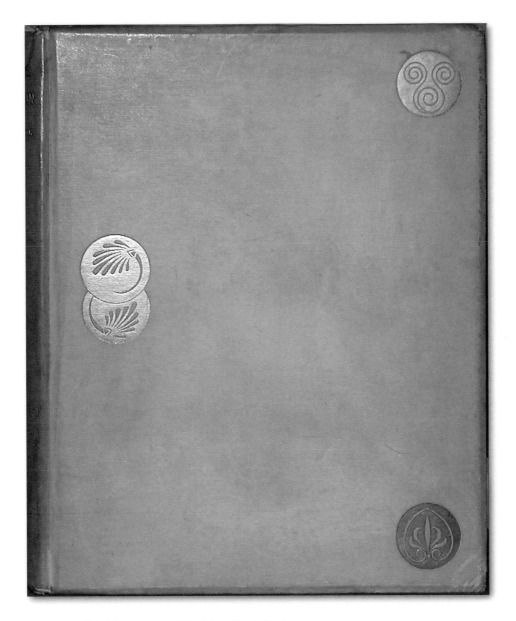

3. Dante Gabriel Rossetti , 1878. *Prince Deukalion* by Bayard Taylor. Boston: Houghton, Osgood and Company; The Riverside Press, Cambridge. 21.9 x 17.6

Smooth cream cloth over beveled boards, having the appearance of vellum, stamped with four gold circles, two of which overlap, each with a different stylized design. This cover design was previously used on Swinburne's *Atalanta in Calydon*, published in London, 1865.

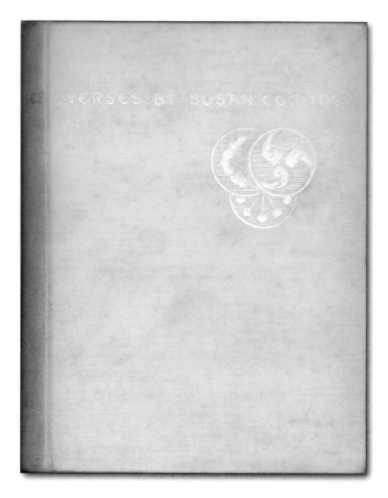

4. Sarah Wyman Whitman, 1880. *Verses* by Susan
Coolidge. Boston: Roberts Brothers. 15.5 x 11.4

Cream cloth stamped in gold with three medallions
overlapping, gold title on cover, gold title and date 1880
on spine. Whitman was among the first fine artists to
design book covers for the publishing industry. This is her
earliest known commercial binding, derived from the style
of Rossetti [3].

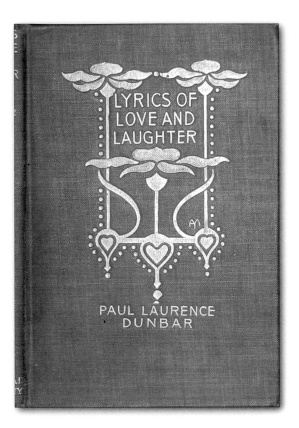

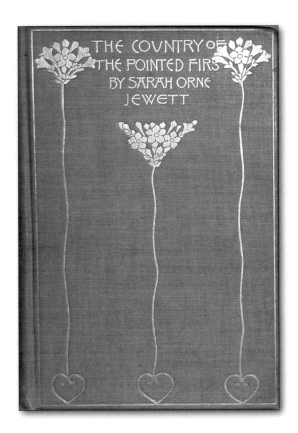

6. Alice Cordelia Morse, 1903. *Lyrics of Love and Laughter* by Paul Laurence Dunbar. New York: Dodd, Mead & Co. This copy issued in 1907. 16.9 x 11.3

Gold-stamped brown cloth. Morse was heavily influenced by Whitman. This is a variant of Morse's 1899 design for Dodd on *My Lady's Slipper*, a collection of poems by Dora Sigerson. It is similar to several designs Whitman did for Houghton Mifflin, including *The Country of the Pointed Firs* (1897, left) and *At The Sign of the Silver Crescent* (1898).

5. Sarah Wyman Whitman, 1897. *The Country of the Pointed Firs* by Sarah Orne Jewett. Boston and New York: Houghton, Mifflin and Company, Cambridge: The Riverside Press. 17.5 x 13.2

Gold-stamped green cloth. Ink inscription "Christmas, 1896." Many books have Christmas inscriptions, indicating they were issued before the year on the title page, as publishers took advantage of the seasonal market. Alice C. Morse was particularly influenced by this design. Compare it to *Lyrics of Love and Laughter* [6].

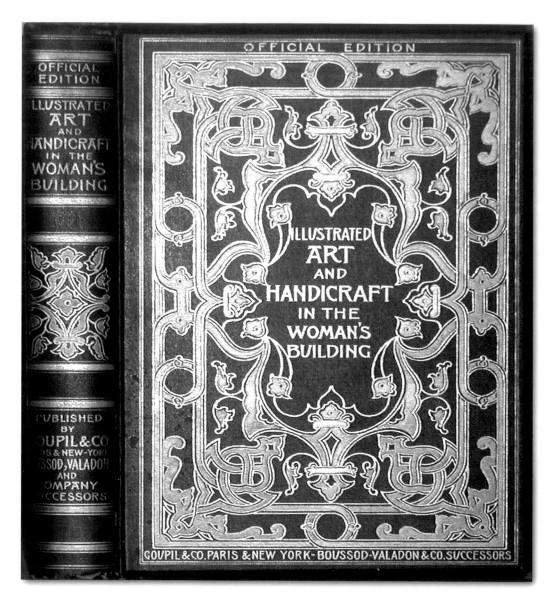

7. Alice Cordelia Morse, 1893. *Art and Handicraft in the Woman's Building.* Maud Howe Elliott, Editor. Goupil & Co. 24.8 x 17.2 [Dubansky Attrib. 93-3]

Black cloth stamped in ornate symmetrical gold and silver design on beveled boards.

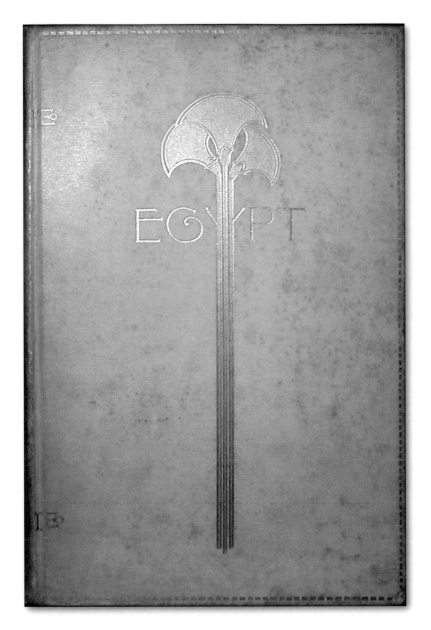

8. Sarah Wyman Whitman, 1892. *Egypt* by Martin Brimmer. Houghton, Mifflin and Company; The Riverside Press, Cambridge, 26.2 x 17.4

Gold-stamped vellum. Also issued in suede with the same design in brown.

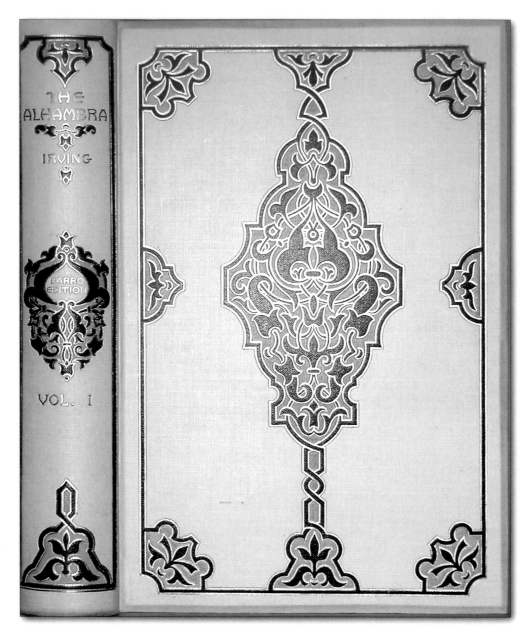

9. Alice C. Morse, 1891. *The Alhambra* by Washington Irving.
New York: G.P. Putnam's Sons; The Knickerbocker Press.
"Darro Edition," two volumes. 22.4 x 16.1

Turquoise, dark blue, and gold on white cloth, issued in cloth
dust jackets and slipcase. This cover evokes Moorish design
(cf. *The Grammar of Ornament*, "Moresque Ornament from the
Alhambra" No. 3).

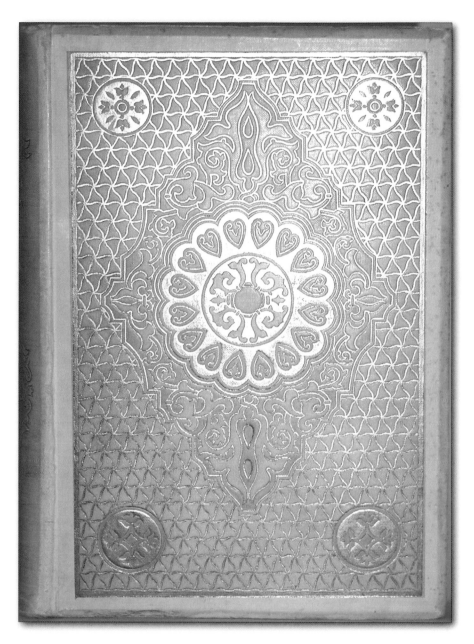

10. Alice C. Morse, 1893. *Chronicle of the Conquest of Granada* by
Washington Irving. New York: G. P. Putnam's Sons; The Knickerbocker Press. "Agapida Edition," two volumes. 22.5 x 14.5

Light pink, aqua, and gold on white cloth. *Granada* adds an Arts
and Crafts touch to a synthesis of Arabic, Moorish, and Persian
ornament. The gold disks in the corners are like the brass bosses
on early European leather bindings, which often had a center
medallion as well.

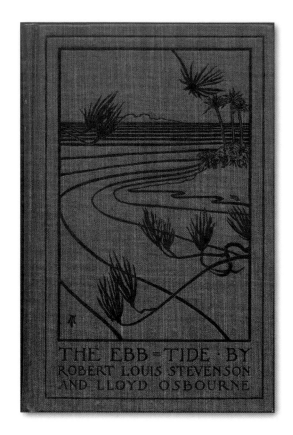

11. Thomas Buford Meteyard, 1894. *The Ebb–Tide: A Trio and Quartette* by Robert Louis Stevenson and Lloyd Osbourne. Chicago & Cambridge: Stone & Kimball. 17.7 x 11.4

Green cloth with gold title on spine, dark green line art of stylized tidal beach on front cover, single line border on back cover. In this deceptively simple line drawing, the illusion of depth is heightened by curves like those on a topographic map. The top of a cloud sits on the horizon, implying the space beyond—or is it an island in the distance?

12. [unknown] , 1898. *Love and Rocks* by Laura E. Richards. Boston: Estes & Lauriat. 17.5 x 11.2

Blue, white, brown, and gold on beige~gray cloth. This anonymous work has a similar compositional structure to Meteyard's cover on *The Ebb–Tide* [11], but anticipates the color sensibilities and spatial relationships of the Art Deco period and serigraphic works of the 1970s. The asymmetrical composition shows a Japanese influence reminiscent of the woodblock seascapes of Hokusai and Hiroshige.

13. Lee Thayer (DD), 1900. *Shadowings* by Lafcadio Hearn.
Boston: Little, Brown & Company. 10.7 x 13

Light blue, blue and gold stamping on dark blue cloth.
Many booksellers list the artist as Bruce Rogers when it is by
Lee Thayer of The Decorative Designers firm. Cover historian
Charles Gullans considered this to be her masterpiece. The
wraparound composition breaks into bordered panels on
front, back, and spine, but the lotus pads are rendered in
the cloth color, as is the border, creating continuity. This is a
photograph of the second (1901) printing.

14. Maud Hunt Squire & E. Mars , 1902. *The Adventures of Ulysses*
by Charles Lamb. Illustrated by Maud Hunt Squire & E. Mars.
New York: R. H. Russell. 24.5 x 19.2

Black and tan stamping on purple cloth. An ancient Greek ship is
tossed by waves reminiscent of a Japanese woodcut.

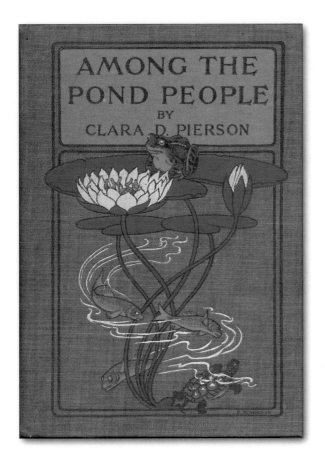

15. F. C. Gordon , 1901. *Among the Pond People* by Clara D. Pierson. New York: E.P. Dutton and Company. 19.8 x 13.4

Orange, white, dark green, and purple pond scene on green cloth. The turtle has one foot on the border of the picture and the lotus pads pierce the sides of it, advancing these elements in front of the picture plane. This creates an illusion of depth, and evokes a feeling of rising from the water. This is similar to an inhabited initial letter of the Renaissance, with the turtle using the border as a prop. The influence of Japanese woodcuts is seen in the flow of the composition.

16. William Snelling Hadaway, 1897. *Prisoners of Conscience: A Story of Shetland* by Amelia Barr. Illustrations by Louis Loeb. New York: The Century Co., 1897. 19.7 x 13.5

Gray cloth with front cover image of a ship in a rough sea stamped in black, seen through a window, silhouetted against an orange sun in a gold sky.

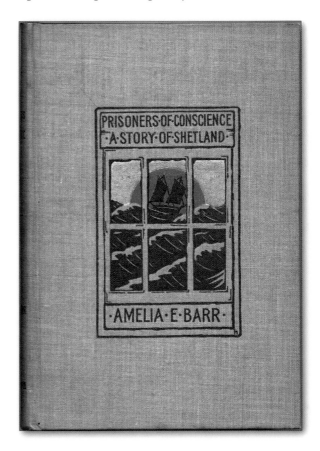

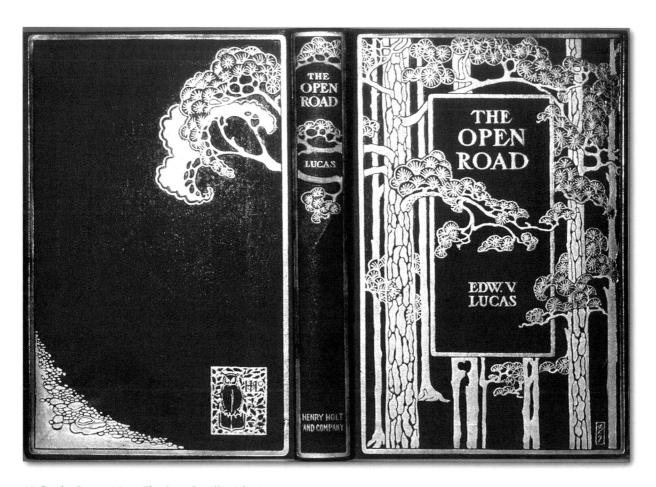

17. Bertha Stuart, 1905. *The Open Road* by Edw. V.
Lucas. New York: Henry Holt and Company. 16 x 10.7

One of Bertha Stuart's most interesting cover designs was
produced with simplicity, using two-tone gold (stamped
with one textured die) on red cloth over thin, flexible
boards. The branches move both behind and in front of
the title plane, a device Stuart used many times. Compare
this to the title box in her 1911 design for Bobbs-Merrill
on Tennyson's *The Princess* [18]. Holt issued a series of
books in this format, all with different bindings by Stuart.
Each title was produced in both red and green cloth.

18. Bertha Stuart, 1911. *The Princess* by Alfred, Lord
Tennyson. Illustrated by Howard Chandler Christy.
[Indianapolis]: The Bobbs-Merrill Company. 29.2 x 22.8

Pink and green floral design with gold title on dark olive
cloth, blindstamped title on spine.

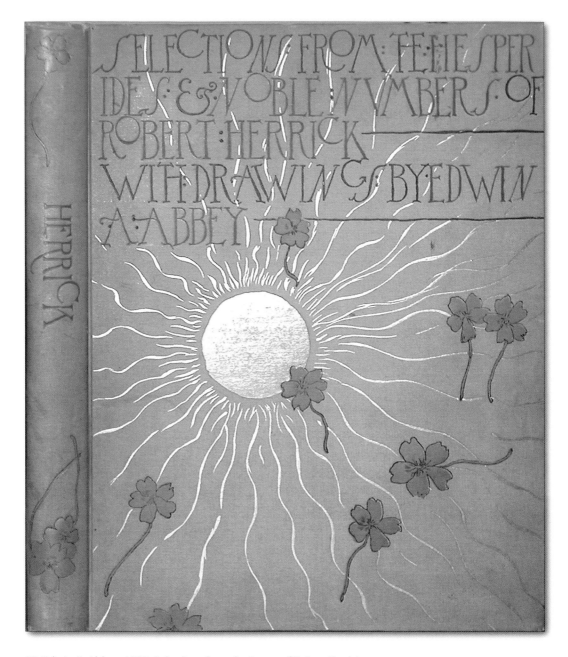

19. Edwin A. Abbey, 1882. *Selections from the Poetry of Robert Herrick.*
Drawings by Edwin A. Abbey. New York: Harper & Brothers. 35 x 24

Gold, red, black, and pea-green on straw-colored cloth. A continuation of
Abbey's development of an Art Nouveau style, first seen the previous year
on his cover for du Chaillu's *The Land of the Midnight Sun* (p. 12). On this
cover Abbey added title lettering, but it appears almost as an afterthought.
Compare this to [20] on the facing page.

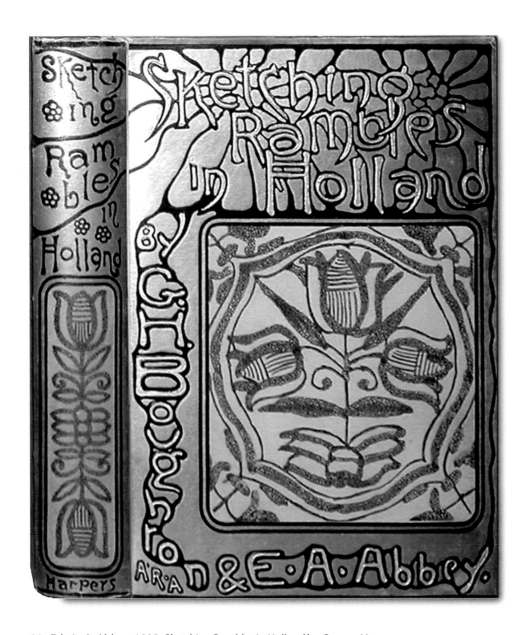

20. Edwin A. Abbey, 1885. *Sketching Rambles in Holland* by George H. Boughton. Illustrated by George H. Boughton & Edwin A. Abbey. New York: Harper & Brothers. 23.7 x 17.5

Gold, black, silver, and gray on a light hay-colored cloth, with blind stamping on the back cover. The gold covers so much of the cloth that it creates the illusion of gold cloth with an inlaid panel. Abbey's development of Art Nouveau is in full flower here, with organic lettering taking a dominant place in the composition. The background of gold stylized flowers extends from the front cover across the spine.

21. Will Bradley, 1894. *In Russet & Silver* by Edmund Gosse. Chicago: Stone & Kimball. 17.8 x 11.5

Russet and silver-stamped tan buckram. Bradley wrapped the art around the book in an unusual way. The forest scene appears to be continuous from the front cover across the spine to the back, but in fact the front and back cover images are identical, with the spine treatment bridging them. The landscape is reduced to abstract silhouettes, yet retains a naturalistic feeling. The trees are the color of the cloth, requiring only two colors for production. The title floats in front of the image in silver.

   Prior to Bradley, cover artists created the illusion of pictorial depth with perspective drawing. The use of color in flat planes to create depth of field was a significant change in concept. The trees are on the picture plane, with two other planes, the mountains and the sky, receding behind the trees. The silver title and sky squeeze the image into a flatter space. Decades later Hans Hofmann used "push and pull" of the picture plane as a central concept in his art and teaching.

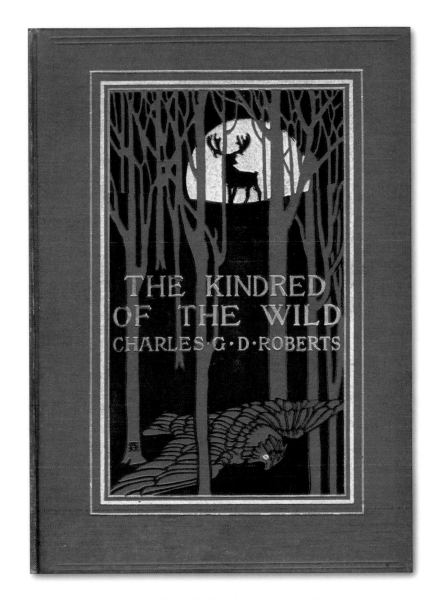

22. Amy M. Sacker, 1902. *The Kindred Of The Wild: A Book Of Animal Life* by Charles G. D. Roberts. Illustrated by Charles Livingston Bull. Boston: L. C. Page & Company. 20.8 x 14.7

Dark green and gold on green cloth. Silhouetted by a golden moon, the elk on a hill creates a dramatic image behind Bradley-style trees. The gold title advances, creating tension. But below the title Amy Sacker gives a twist to the picture plane, with a gold-eyed owl coming toward us, pulling the space around it forward as it flies between the trees.

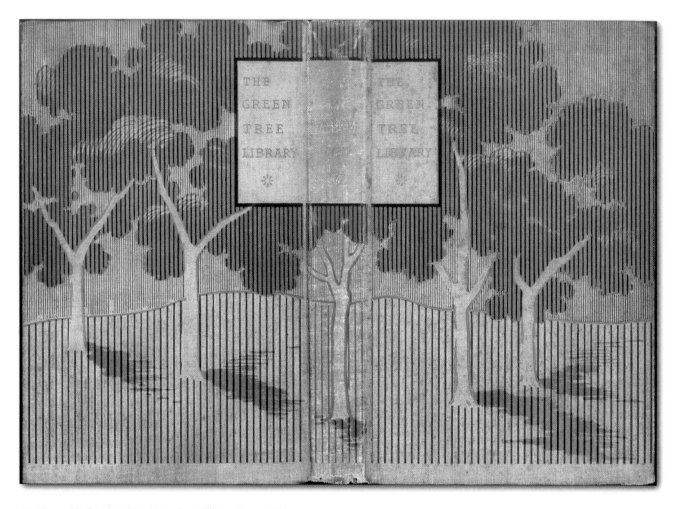

23. Henry McCarter, 1894. *Vistas* by William Sharp. Chicago: Stone & Kimball. No. 1 in the Green Tree Library series. 17.7 x 11.5

Purple, green, and gold stamping on light green cloth. *Vistas* is a true wraparound design, with different front and back panels. The purple lines create shading with a halftone effect. While Bradley was designing *In Russet & Silver* [21], Henry McCarter created a design for S&K's Green Tree Library series. Each book in the series is a different thickness, and McCarter created a tree for the spine that can be cropped to different widths. McCarter was a student of Thomas Eakins, and in 1894 had just established his own studio in New York, having returned from the École des Beaux-Arts in Paris. There he befriended Toulouse-Lautrec, studied the impressionists, and was inspired by Japanese woodcuts.

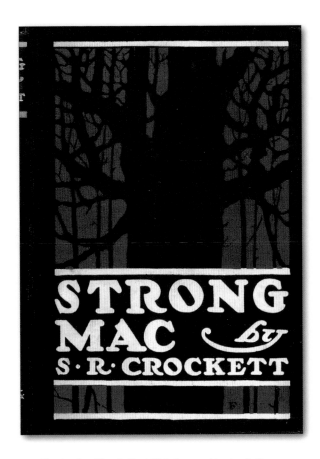

24. Charles Buckles Falls, 1904. *Strong Mac* by S. R. Crockett. Illustrated by Maurice Greiffenhagen. New York: Dodd, Mead and Company. 19.7 x 13.2

Orange and pinkish white on lightly textured black cloth, gold title on spine. C. B. Falls created a dramatic image by silhouetting a close-up view of a bare tree. Several smaller trees are in the background. Is it winter, or are they dead? Instead of running the title over the tree, he broke the image into separate parts. Even though the orange advances on the black picture plane, the title plane lays in front of it, creating depth.

25. Olive Lothrop Grover , 1899. *The Story Without an End* (from the German of Carove) by Sarah Austin. Boston: Dana Estes & Company. 19 x 13.5

Beige cloth stamped in tan, green, and black. Olive Grover's design uses childlike perspective with ambiguous depth and a figure that presages Botero.

26. Charles L. Hinton , 1902. *Under the Trees by* Hamilton Wright Mabie. Illustrated by Charles L. Hinton. New York: Dodd, Mead and Company. 21.9 x 15.2

Black, white, and gold on green cloth. Hinton's synthesis of a Pre-Raphaelite scene with Arts & Crafts lettering and circular frame, tied with an Art Nouveau ribbon.

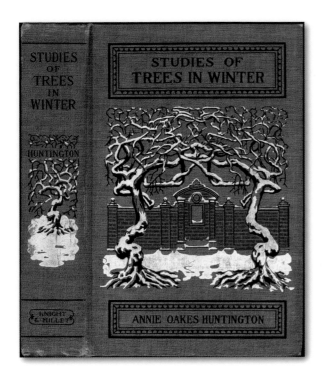

27. [Unknown], 1902. *Studies of Trees in Winter* by Annie Oakes Huntington. Illustrated with colored plates by Mary S. Morse and photographs by the author. Boston: Knight & Millet. 21.3 x 14.5

Blue~gray cloth stamped with black, white, and brick red.

28. Adrian Iorio, 1910. *Studies of Trees in Winter* by Annie Oakes Huntington. Illustrated with colored plates by Mary S. Morse and photographs by the author. Boston: Dana Estes and Company. 21.4 x 14.3

Maroon cloth stamped with black, white, and gray winter scene, white title. When Dana Estes issued the 1910 reprint of this book the firm commissioned a cover from Adrian Iorio, who had worked for Will Bradley. This edition retains the spine image from the 1902 Knight & Millet edition. Whether this indicates a choice by Iorio or a budgetary decision by the publisher is unknown. It is possible that Iorio created the earlier cover as well.

29. [Unknown], 1904. *Getting Acquainted with the Trees* by J. Horace McFarland.
Illustrated with photographs by the author. New York: The Outlook Company.
22.1 x 16.6

Light turquoise green flat-weave cloth stamped with dark green tree in a field, the
design wrapping the spine and 3 mm onto the back cover. The lettering is stamped
in gold with a black outline. The tree design has almost no impression and sits near
the surface of the cloth. At first glance the tree silhouette looks photographic, but
the loosely sketched environment around it sets a counterpoint that demands a
second look at the drawing. The depth of stamping of the gold sits well behind the
cloth plane of the treescape, yet the lettering appears to float in front.

30. Frank Hazenplug, 1913. *The Jungle Book* by Rudyard Kipling. Illustrated by M. and E. Detmold. New York: The Century Company. 21.4 x 14.7

Light turquoise, moss green, and gold on olive-green cloth. A remarkable design in which the gold seems to light up the forest, like sunlight filtering through the trees. One tree uses the cloth color as a silhouette, along with the foreground figures of a boy and wolf. The colors of the trees lighten as they recede, aiding the illusion that they are closer to the source of light.

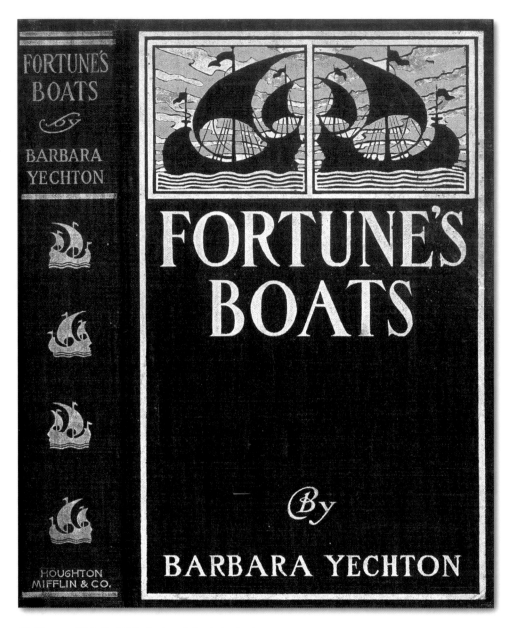

31. Thomas W. Ball , 1900. *Fortune's Boats* by Barbara
Yechton. Boston and New York: Houghton, Mifflin and
Company; The Riverside Press, Cambridge. 20.1 x 13.1

Blue cloth with mirrored sailing vessel silhouetted in gold
and silver.

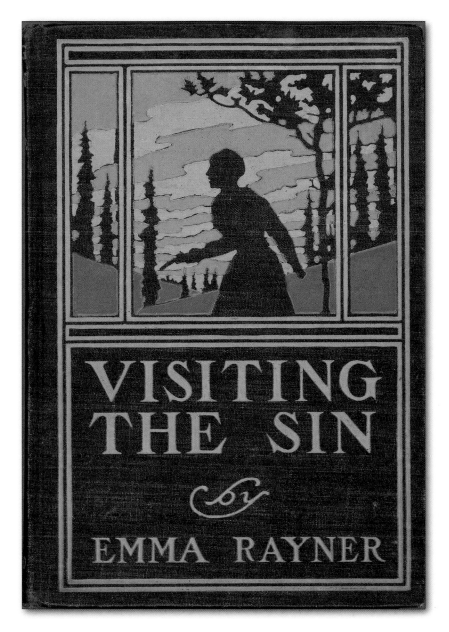

32. Thomas W. Ball , 1900. *Visiting the Sin* by Emma
Rayner. Boston: Small, Maynard & Company. 19.8 x 13.5

Gray, light blue, and cream pictorial of woman with a
gun on gray~green cloth.

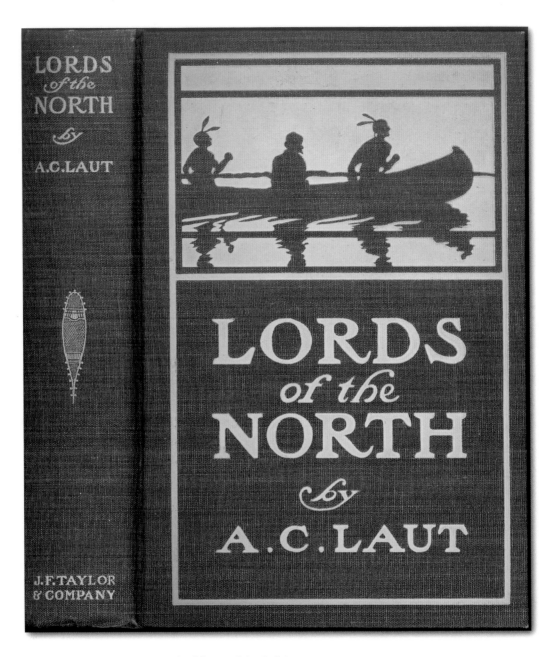

33. Thomas W. Ball, 1900. *Lords of the North* by A. C. Laut.
New York: J. F. Taylor & Company. 20.1 x 13.7

Green cloth stamped with cream silhouette of Indians
paddling a canoe, cream title on cover and spine, gold
snowshoe on spine.

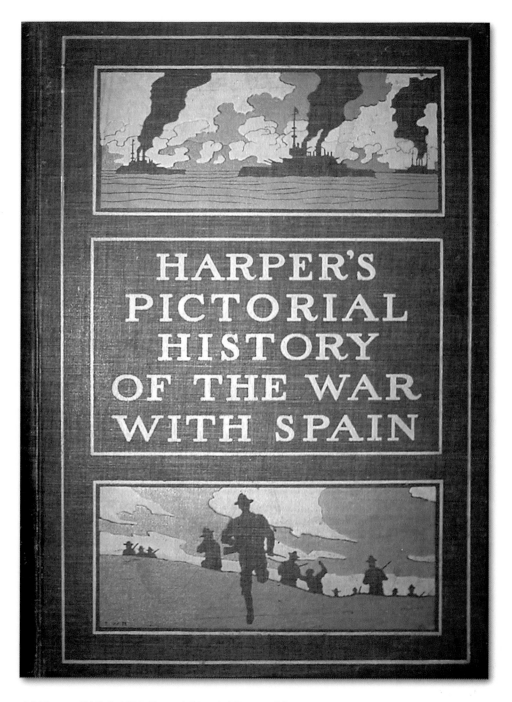

34. Thomas W. Ball, 1899. *Harper's Pictorial History of the War with Spain*. Introduction by Maj.-Gen. Nelson A. Miles. New York and London: Harper & Brothers. 41.8 x 29.5

Gray cloth stamped in yellow, green, brown and gold.

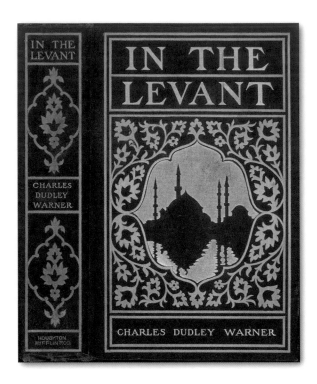

35. Thomas W. Ball, 1901. *In The Levant* by Charles Dudley Warner. Boston and New York: Houghton, Mifflin and Company. 20.2 x 13.2

Dark green cloth stamped in light gray~green and gold.

36. Thomas W. Ball, 1903. *Castilian Days* by John Hay. Illustrated by Joseph Pennell. Boston and New York: Houghton, Mifflin and Company; The Riverside Press, Cambridge. 20.2 x 13.2

Dark green cloth stamped in green, gray, yellow~green, bright gold, and multitextured matte gold.

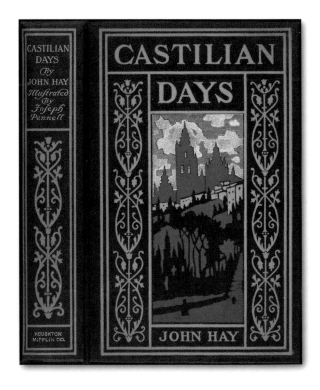

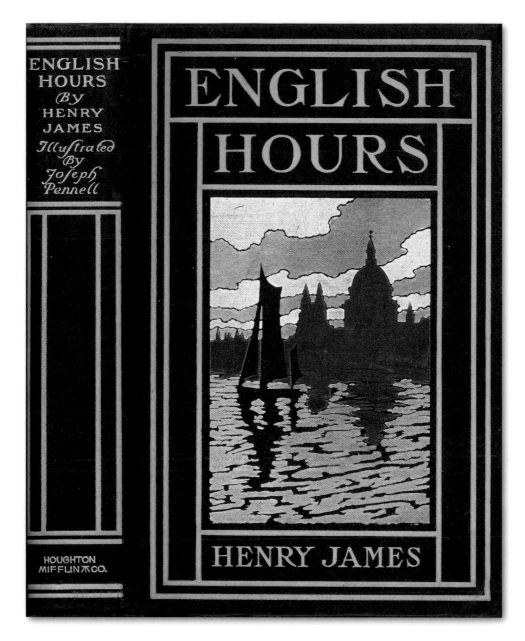

37. Thomas W. Ball, 1905. *English Hours* by Henry James.
Illustrated by Joseph Pennell. Boston and New York: Houghton,
Mifflin and Company; The Riverside Press, Cambridge. 21 x 13.6

Charcoal black cloth stamped with gray, bright gold, and matte
gold scene of a sailboat on the water with skyline and clouds.
Title and line borders in greenish yellow on cover, title in gold
on spine. Often wrongly attributed to Bruce Rogers, who did the
typographic design for this book.

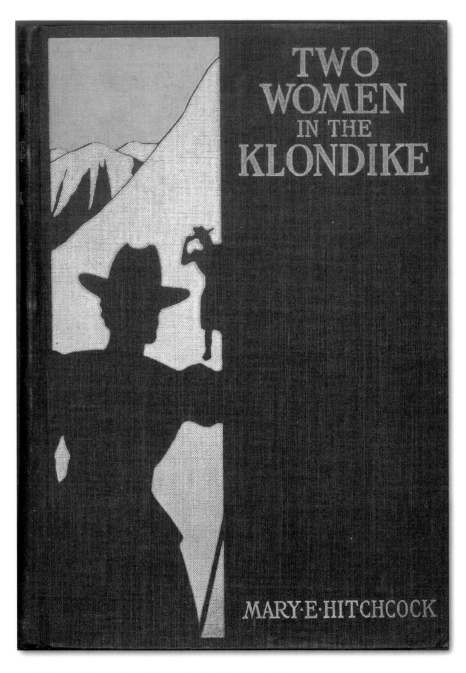

38. [Unknown], 1899. *Two Women in the Klondike* by Mary
E. Hitchcock. G. P. Putnam's Sons; The Knickerbocker Press.
22.5 x 15.5

Dark gray cloth stamped in light gray and yellow with scene
of two silhouetted women on a snow-covered mountain,
gold title.

39. [Unknown], 1915. *Daybreak* by Elizabeth Miller. New York: Charles Scribner's Sons. 19.5 x 13.3

Dark teal~gray cloth with sailing ship silhouetted against an orange sky with gold rising sun and gold reflections on waves.

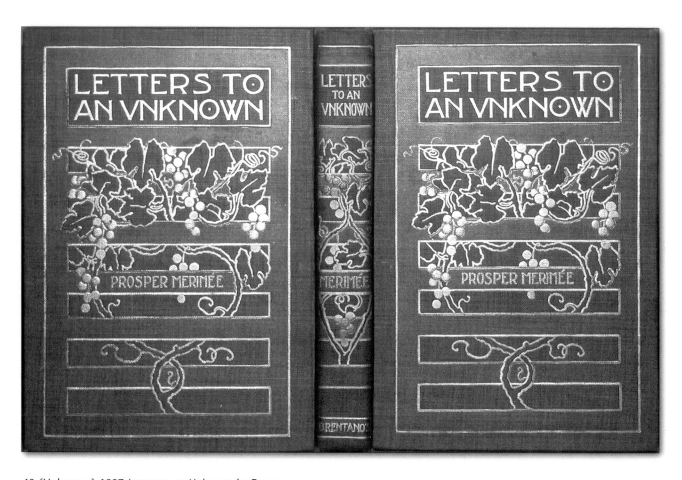

40. [Unknown], 1897. *Letters to an Unknown* by Prosper Mérimée, translated with a Preface by Henri Pène du Bois. New York, Chicago, Washington, Paris: Brentano's. 18.2 x 12.5

Beige cloth deeply stamped with matte varnish, overstamped with gold grapevine and title on both covers and spine. An unusual spatial effect created by weaving the image in and out of the panel, with a semi-matte varnish or similar finish either stencilled or printed in an area around the panels. At some viewing angles the finish disappears, at others it is reflective. Some of this effect was captured by adjusting the lighting for the photograph.

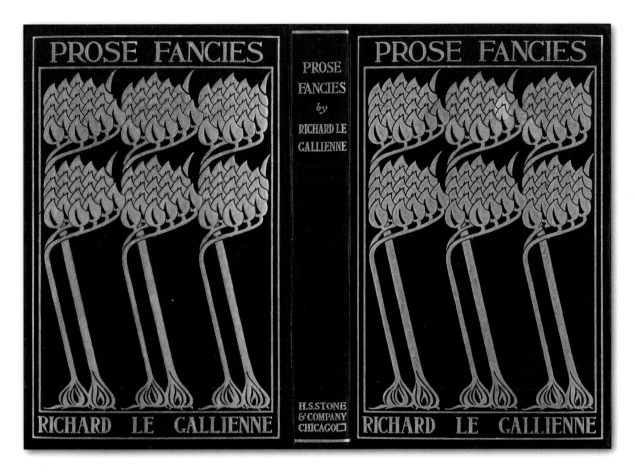

41. Frank Hazenplug, 1896. *Prose Fancies* by Richard Le Gallienne.
Chicago and London: Herbert S. Stone & Co.; John Lane. 17.6 x 11.3

Repeat pattern of six stylized plants (Gullans says "perhaps the most
beautiful artichokes ever seen in the nineteenth century") on maroon
cloth stamped in gold. Same on both covers; gold title on cover and
spine.

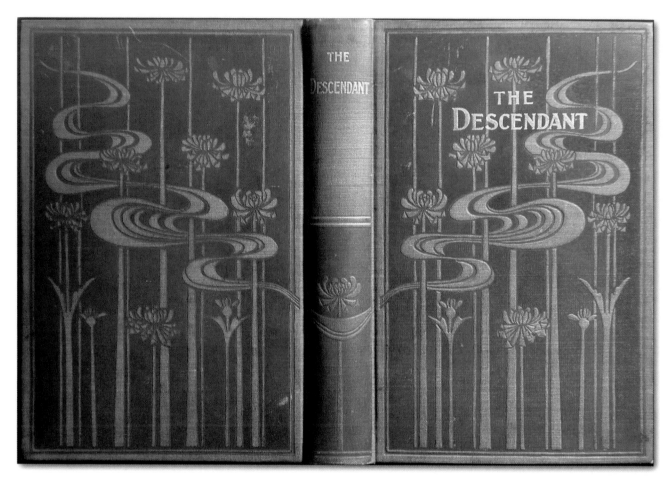

42. [Unknown], 1897. *The Descendant* by Ellen Glasgow.
New York and London: Harper & Brothers. 19 x 12.7

Beige~gray cloth stamped with green wraparound mirror-image Art Nouveau panelized floral design. The binding on this first issue of Glasgow's first novel did not identify the author.

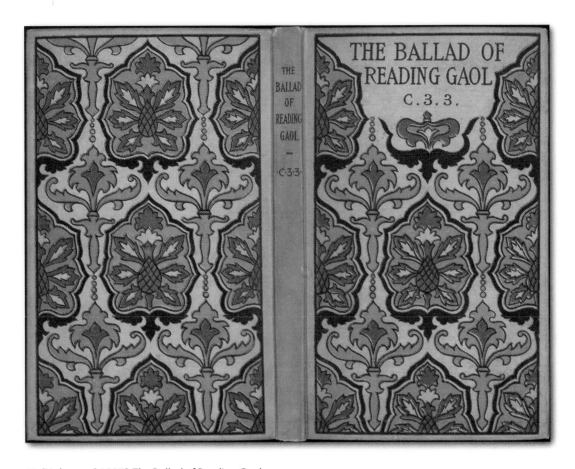

43. [Unknown] 1897? *The Ballad of Reading Gaol*
by C. 3. 3. (Oscar Wilde). New York: Brentano's.
16.0 x 10.0

Tan cloth stamped in orange, olive, and black. C. 3. 3.
was Wilde's cell number. He wrote this in 1897 when
he was released from Reading Gaol after two years of
imprisonment for homosexual acts.

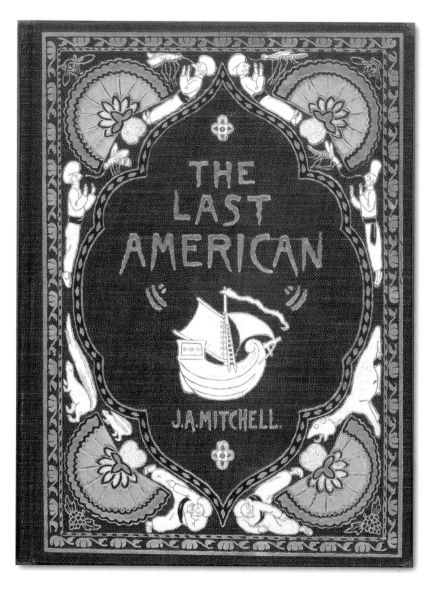

44. Albert D. Blashfield, 1902. *The Last American*
by J. A. Mitchell. Illustrations by F. W. Read and the
author, decorations by Albert D. Blashfield. New York:
Frederick A. Stokes Company. 19.6 x 14.4

Blue cloth stamped in red, white, yellow, and gold.

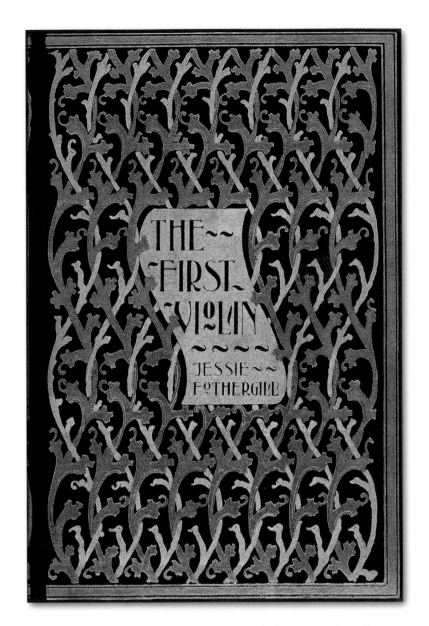

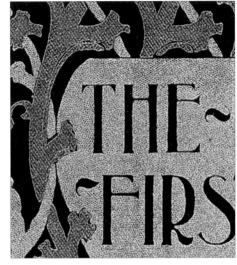

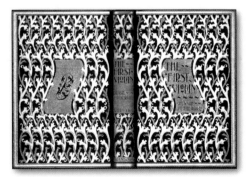

45. Lee and Henry Thayer (?), 1896. *The First Violin* by Jessie Fothergill.
Illustrated by G.W. Brenneman. New York: Brentano's. 21 x 13.8

Two volume set in two-tone gold on black cloth, issued in cloth dust
jackets and a slipcase. As you turn the book in your hand, different
parts are illuminated. The effect is caused by a stamping die engraved
or etched with textures that reflect at different angles. The enlarged
detail shows the technique. The small photo of the book shows how it
changes with different lighting, as well as the way the border is used to
tie the front and back covers into a single design.

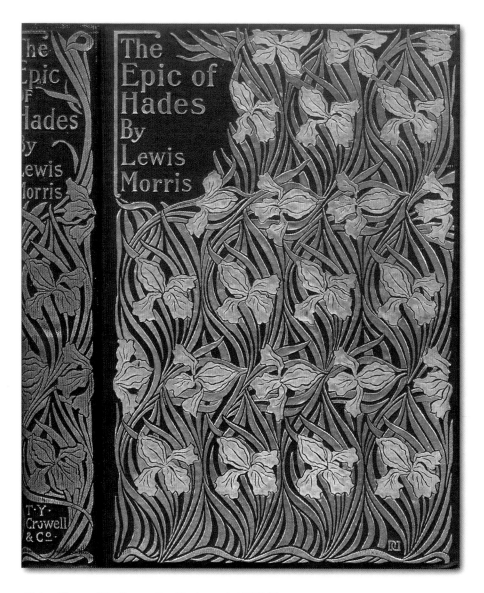

46. Lee Thayer (The Decorative Designers), 1897? *The Epic of Hades* by Lewis Morris. New York and Boston: Thomas Y. Crowell and Company. 17.3 x 11.7

Two-tone (textured die) repeating pattern of irises on burgundy cloth. Crowell used the same design on pea-green cloth for *Colomba* by Prosper Mérimée.

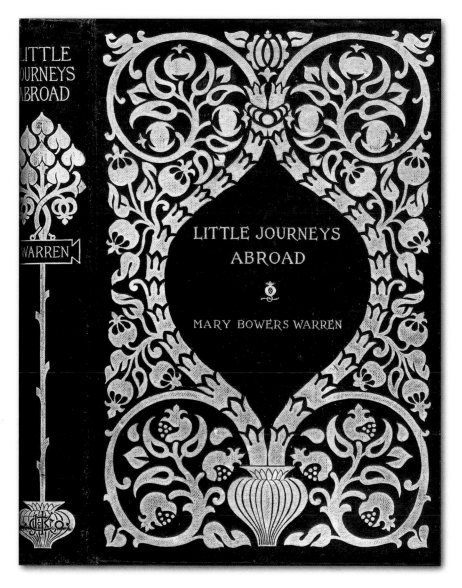

47. Amy M. Sacker , 1895. *Little Journeys Abroad.*
by Mary Bowers Warren. Illustrated by George H.
Boughton, E.K. Johnson, Irving R. Wiles, J.A. Holzer, Will
H. Drake. Boston: Joseph Knight Company. 19 x 13

Gold-stamped dark blue cloth. An Arts and Crafts design
that also shows the influence of Art Nouveau. Compare
it to Amy Richards' 1901 design on *Amos Judd* [(p. 11).

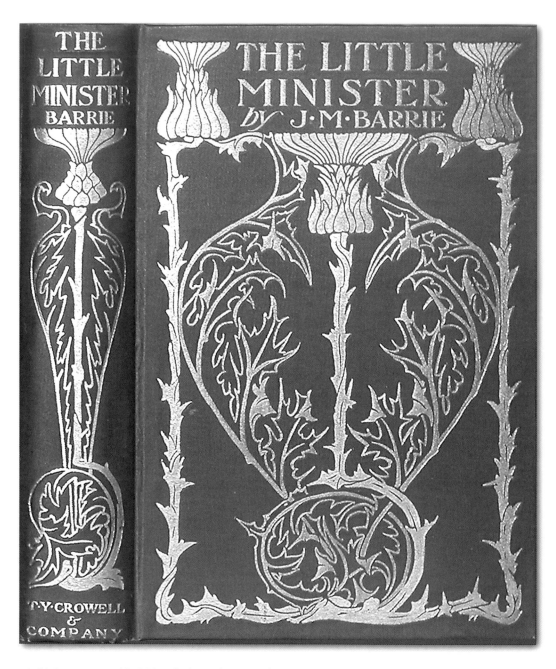

48. [Unknown, possibly DD], n.d. *The Little Minister* by
J. M. Barrie. New York: Thomas Y. Crowell & Company.
Luxembourg Edition. 20.8 x 14.9

Gold-stamped green cloth. Crowell issued many titles as
Luxembourg Editions, each with a different ornate binding,
most of which were by The Decorative Designers.

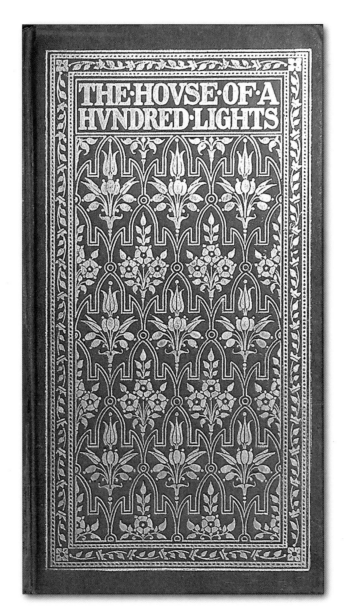

49. Bertram Grosvenor Goodhue, 1900. *The House of a Hundred Lights* by Frederic Ridgely Torrence. Title page and decorations by Bertram Grosvenor Goodhue. Boston: Small Maynard & Company. 18.2 x 9.8

Green paper over boards stamped in gold, back cover stamped with same design in blind.

Margaret Armstrong created a series of covers for Charles Scribner's Sons for a dozen books by Henry Van Dyke published between 1901 and 1926. 19.5 x 13.

Dark blue cloth. All have horizontal symmetry and are stamped in colors and gold. Several of the titles were also issued with the same design in blind or gold-stamped leather. *The Valley of Vision* [52] is stamped in what was then called "Japan" gold, a copper alloy, while the others seen here use true gold leaf. There may have been a shortage of gold when the 1919 edition was being produced, likely for the Christmas 1918 market, at the end of World War I.

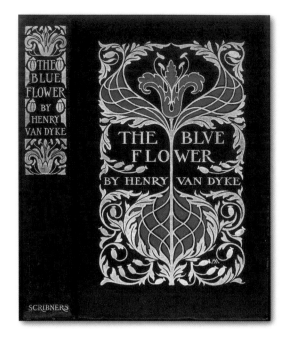

51. *The Blue Flower*, 1902.

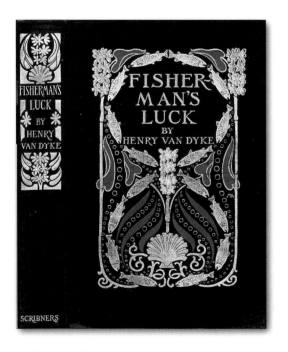

50. *Fisherman's Luck,* 1905.

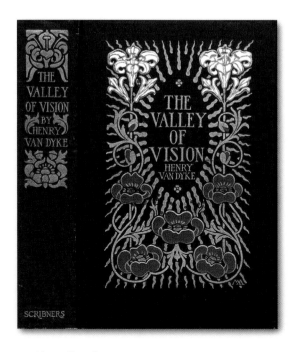

52. *The Valley of Vision*, 1919.

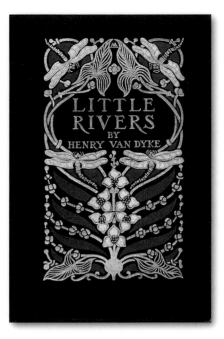

54. *Little Rivers,* 1903.

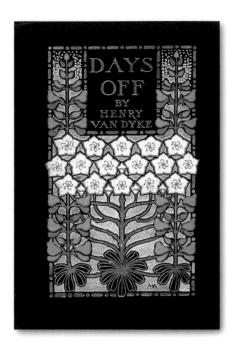

55. *Days Off,* 1907.

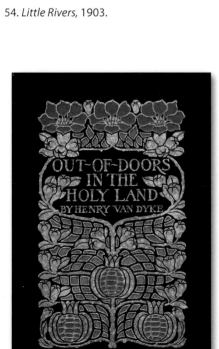

56. *Out-of-Doors in the Holy Land,* 1908.

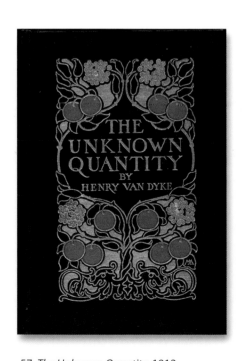

57. *The Unknown Quantity,* 1912.

58. Margaret Armstrong, 1900. *Pippa Passes* by Robert Browning. Illustrated by Margaret Armstrong. New York: Dodd, Mead & Co. 22.4 x 15

Pink, brown, bright and matte gold stamping on olive green cloth with white cloth onlay. White stamping flaked notoriously before 1901. A cloth onlay enabled bright white to be used in the composition.

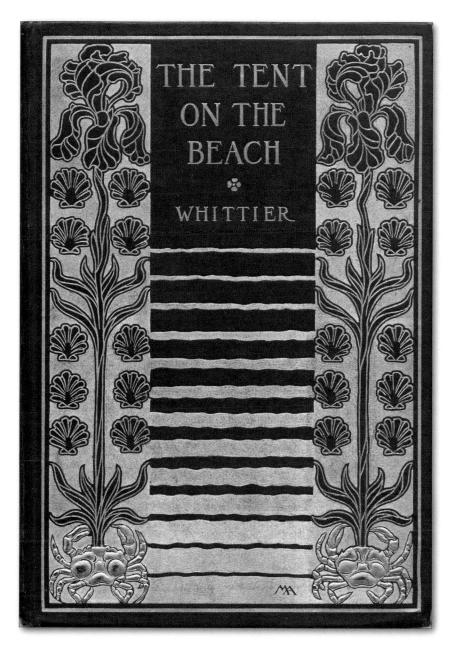

59. Margaret Armstrong, 1890. *The Tent on the Beach*
by John Greenleaf Whittier. Illustrated by Charles H.
Woodbury and Marcia O. Woodbury. Boston and New
York: Houghton, Mifflin and Company; The Riverside
Press, Cambridge. 20.2 x 14.2

Maroon cloth stamped in gold. Also issued in green cloth.

Rather than have one artist create all the covers for a single author, as Scribner's did for Van Dyke (pp. 66-67), Dodd, Mead commissioned different artists for the covers of their top authors. On this page are three books written by Paul Leicester Ford.

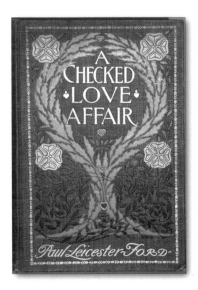

60. George Wharton Edwards, 1903. *A Checked Love Affair* and *The Cortelyou Feud*. Illustrated by Harrison Fisher. 22.3 x 14.9

Sea green, dark green, white, and gold on green cloth.

61. Thomas Maitland Cleland, 1906. *A Warning to Lovers*. Illustrated by Henry Hutt, decorations by T. M. Cleland. 22.4 x 14.6

Gold stamped and embossed blue~gray cloth.

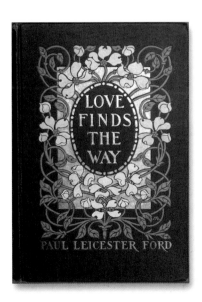

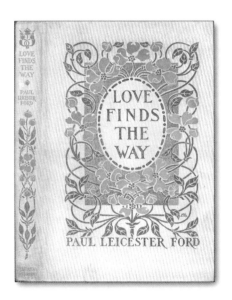

62. and 63. Margaret Armstrong, 1904. *Love Finds the Way*. Illustrated by Harrison Fisher, decorations by Margaret Armstrong. 22.4 x 15.7

Several variants were issued. At left is the common copy in light green, white and gold on green cloth. Above, a scarce copy in green, pink, and gold on cream diagonally ribbed cloth.

The first widely read African-American poet was Paul Laurence Dunbar. His first book was self-published and sold from his job as an elevator operator. Dodd, Mead signed him on and hired some of the best artists to create covers for their editions.

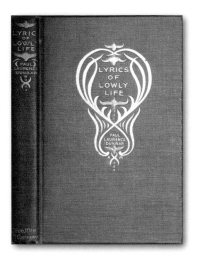

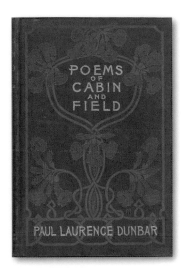

64. Alice C. Morse. 1896. *Lyrics of Lowly Life.* 17 x 11

Gold-stamped olive green cloth. This was the first Dunbar title issued by Dodd, Mead, and was reprinted several times with the same binding. Above is the 1897 edition.

65. Alice C. Morse, 1900. *Poems of Cabin and Field.* Photographs by the Hampton Institute Camera Club, decorations by Alice C. Morse. 22.4 x 15

Orange, turquoise, and gold on green cloth.

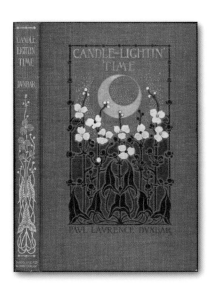

66. Margaret Armstrong, 1901. *Candle-Lightin' Time.* Photographs by the Hampton Institute Camera Club, decorations by Margaret Armstrong. 22.3 x 15

Maroon, white, dark green, and gold on green cloth.

67. [Unknown], 1906. *Joggin' Erlong.* Photographs by Leigh Richmond Miner, decorations by John Rae. 22.3 x 14.8

Red paisley cloth with paper spine label and paper front cover label with photograph. This "bandanna" binding captured the feeling of Dunbar's poetry.

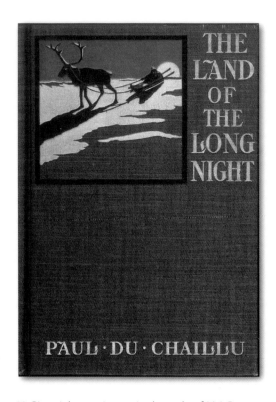

68. Pictorial cover image in the style of M.J. Burns, lettering style of Henry Thayer, 1899. *The Land of the Long Night* by Paul du Chaillu. Illustrated by M. J. Burns. New York: Charles Scribner's Sons. 20.3 x 14

Gray~green cloth with gray~blue, off white, and black image of a reindeer pulling a sled in the moonlight, gold title on front cover and spine.

69. [Unknown, likely George W. Hood], 1902. *The River* by Eden Phillpotts. New York: Frederick A. Stokes Company. 19 x 12.3

Slate blue and white stamping of moonlit riverscape on midnight blue cloth.

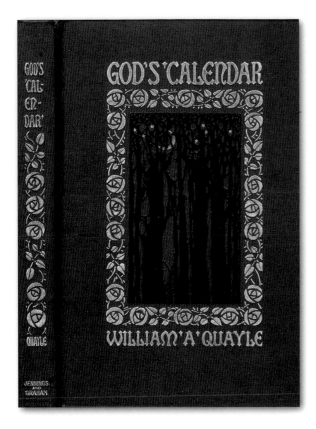

70. [Unknown], 1907. *God's Calendar* by William A. Quayle. Cincinnati and New York: Jennings and Graham, Eaton and Mains. 23.6 x 16.1

Black and gold on green cloth. Once again Will Bradley's flat trees establish the foreground, but this time they are stamped in black, with the cloth color for the background. There is no landscape before the sky, just deep space with the gold crescent moon and stars seen through the branches.

71. Frank Hazenplug, 1910. *Murder Point* by Coningsby W. Dawson. New York: Hodder & Stoughton; George H. Doran Company, 19.4 x 13.1

Black, white and blind stamped pictorial of treescape with stream on moonlit night, magenta title, on olive green vertically ribbed cloth. An unusual use of blind stamping for the sky and water, creating dimensional relief for the treeline silhouette and foreground land. The flattened cloth grain makes the sky feel deeper, and the reflection of the moonlight on the water more liquid. The title advances on the picture plane, adding an illusion of depth to the image.

72. Edward Stratton Holloway, 1903. *At the Time Appointed* by A. Maynard Barbour. Frontispiece by J. N. Marchand. Philadelphia and London: J. B. Lippincott Company. Sixth Edition. 19.8 x 13.3

Red cloth stamped with dark green trees and gold title on cover and spine.

73. [Unknown], 1924. *New England Highways and Byways from a Motor Car* by Thomas D. Murphy. Illustrations from paintings, photographs, and a map. Boston: L.C. Page & Company. 24.5 x 16.3

White, blue, and gold on dark green vertically ribbed cloth.

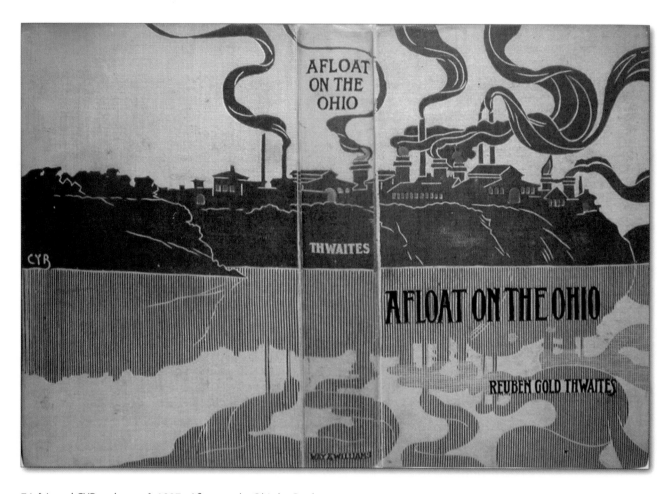

74. [signed CYR, unknown], 1897. *Afloat on the Ohio* by Reuben Gold Thwaites. Chicago: Way & Williams. 19.5 x 12.6

Dark cyan and tan stamping of industrial landscape with black lettering on beige cloth. Author's name and artist's monogram are in drop-out lettering.

75. The Decorative Designers, 1910. *The Holy Land* by Robert
Hichens. Illustrated by Jules Guérin and by photographs.
New York: The Century Company. 27 x 18

A Persian border evokes the geographic region covered in the
text. A tour-de-force of stamping, the cover combines decorative and pictorial elements in seven colors and gold.

76. Thomas W. Ball, 1899. *The Goodness of St. Rocque* by Alice Dunbar. New York: Dodd, Mead and Company. 17.5 x 11.6

Silver and dark green stamping on green cloth.

77. [Unsigned, likely The Decorative Designers], 1897. *The Old Santa Fé Trail* by Colonel Henry Inman. Illustrated by Frederick Remington. Initials and tail pieces by Thomson Willing. Fold-out map. New York: The Macmillan Company. This copy is the fourth printing, January 1898. 22.7 x 15.7

Yellow, maroon, and dark green cactus in abstract landscape with gold title on green cloth.

78. Henry Hunt Clark , 1914. *California: The Land of the Sun* by Mary
Austin. Illustrated by Sutton Palmer. New York: The Macmillan
Company. 24.1 x 19.4

Gold and multicolor stamping on olive green cloth. This elaborate
production looks almost like an oil painting on the cover of the book.

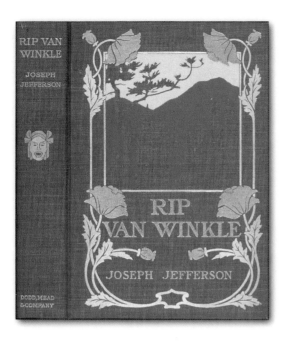

79. Thomas W. Ball, 1899. *Rip Van Winkle* by Joseph Jefferson. Dodd, Mead & Company. 21.3 x 16.3

Green cloth with bright and matte gold decorations and title surrounding a landscape with light blue sky, purple mountains, and trees in the cloth color.

80. [Unsigned, possibly The Decorative Designers], 1900. *Unknown Switzerland* by Victor Tissot. New York: James Pott & Co. 20.5 x 14.2

Multitoned gold, pink, white, lavender, light and dark green stamping on gray cloth.

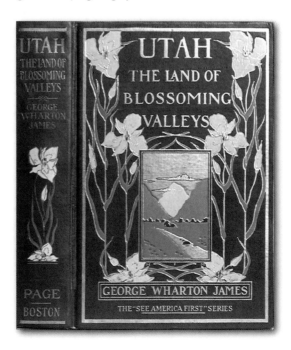

81. Blanche McManus Mansfield, 1922? *Utah: The Land of Blossoming Valleys* by George Wharton James. Boston: The Page Company. 24.5 x 16.4

Pink, purple, green and gold on brown cloth. Stylistically similar to the 1899 and 1900 covers above, this may have been done years earlier than the 1922 publication date.

82. [Unknown], 1880. *Aboard The Mavis* by Richard Markham.
New York: Dodd, Mead and Company. 21.1 x 17.3

Printed paper over boards and cloth spine. A proto-Futurist
composition from the artist who did the Bodley books for
Houghton [1, frontispiece].

83. Florence Lundborg, 1904. *Yosemite Legends* by Bertha H. Smith. Illustrated by Florence Lundborg. San Francisco: Paul Elder and Company. 24.8 x 16.6

Russet cloth with a landscape of black trees and a white waterfall, surrounded by a border of black and white totemic heads. The heads, extended, are used as a repeat pattern for the endpapers and one is in black on the spine. The title is in gold on the cover and spine. The border is based on Native American design, with an Arts and Crafts influence. The abstract composition exhibits a fluidly poetic view of space that evokes the landscapes of Albert Pinkham Ryder and Wassily Kandinsky.

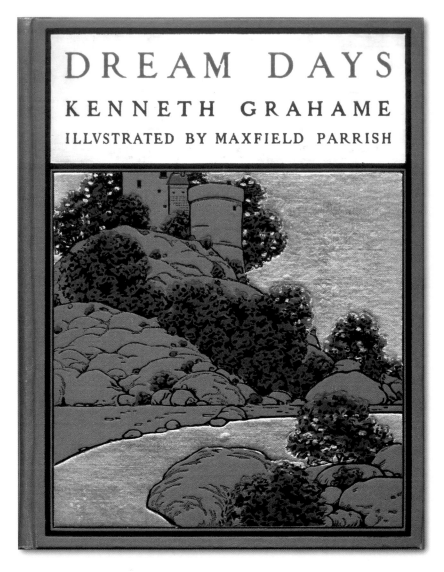

84. Maxfield Parrish, 1902. *Dream Days* by Kenneth Grahame. Illustrated by Maxfield Parrish. London and New York: John Lane, The Bodley Head. 20.7 x 15.7

Black, white, red~orange, green and gold on taupe cloth. Parrish applied his formidable skill as a master of illusionist illustration to this cover, with a dreamlike use of gold, detailed imagery, and flat space. The shrubbery pops off the image plane, where the rocks sit flat as line art—a very modern use of the material to flip our perception back and forth from the image to the surface. The effect is created with technical virtuosity. The gold is visible between the leaves. The black is stamped over the gold, which holds tight edges. The three-dimensional aspect is heightened by the use of detailed shading in the plate that creates highlights by changing the texture of the cloth at the tree tips. The same design was used on the reissue of Grahame's *The Golden Age* as a companion volume.

85. Walter King Stone, 1906. *The Log of the Sun* by C. William Beebe. Illustrated by Walter King Stone. New York: Henry Holt & Company. 25.3 x 18.8

Blue, light green, and gold stamping on dark green cloth.

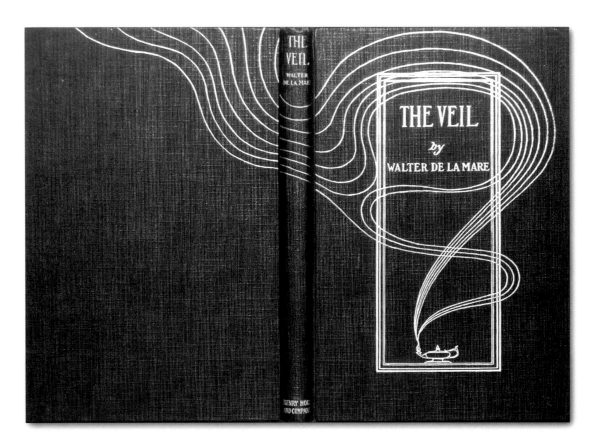

86. [Unknown], 1922 .*The Veil* by Walter de la Mare.
New York: Henry Holt and Company. 22.6 x 15.3

Dark gray cloth stamped with gold "magic lamp" design.
The stylized smoke wraps to the spine and back cover.

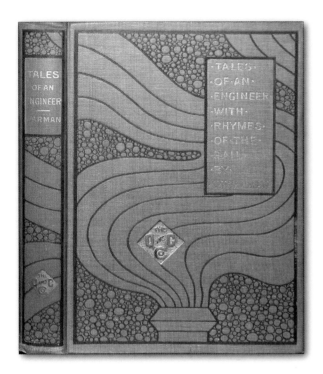

87. [Unsigned], 1895. *Tales of an Engineer with Rhymes of the Rail* by Cy Warman. New York: Charles Scribner's Sons. 18.3 x 12.5.

Pinkish-gray cloth stamped on front cover and spine with maroon smoke coming from a smokestack, gold titles. This copy of the 1896 printing has a diamond-shaped logo "The Q and C Co." stamped on the front cover and spine. The logo does not appear on all copies. Q and C Co. was a Chicago manufacturing company whose products included railroad supplies.

88. Elihu Vedder, 1884. *The Rubáiyát of Omar Khayyám*, Edward Fitzgerald, translator. Illustrated by Elihu Vedder. Boston: Houghton Mifflin and Company; The Riverside Press, Cambridge. 21.5 x 16.3

Maroon and gold stamping on brown cloth. The photo is of the third iteration of this design, 1894. The first was a folio issued in 1884.

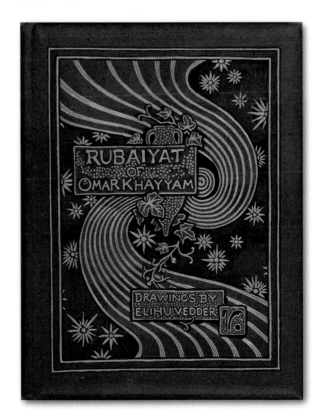

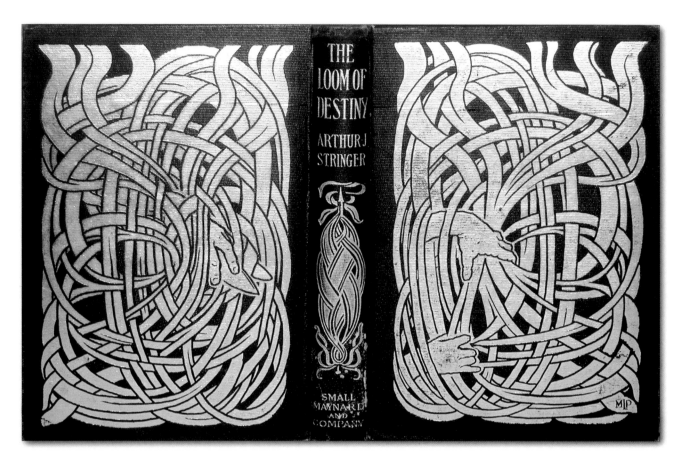

89. Marion L Peabody, 1899. *The Loom of Destiny* by
Arthur J. Stringer. Boston: Small, Maynard & Company.
17.3 x 11.7

Black cloth stamped with silver (white metal) design of
hands and abstract interwoven pattern.

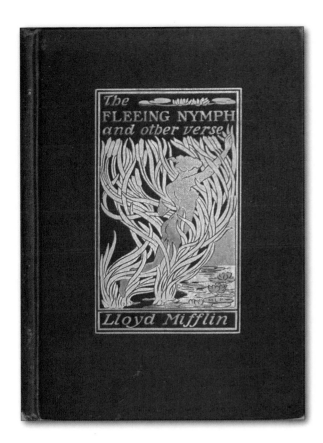

90. Marion L. Peabody, 1905. *The Fleeing Nymph* by Lloyd Mifflin. Boston: Small, Maynard & Company. 19.9 x 13.3

Red cloth stamped in three tones of textured gold with a nymph fleeing through reeds in a pond.

91. Marion L Peabody, 1910. *The Up Grade* by Wilder Goodwin. Illustrations by Charles Grunwald. Boston: Little, Brown and Company. 19.7 x 13.2

Teal cloth stamped in black and gold image of a man with his sleeve rolled up, holding a staff.

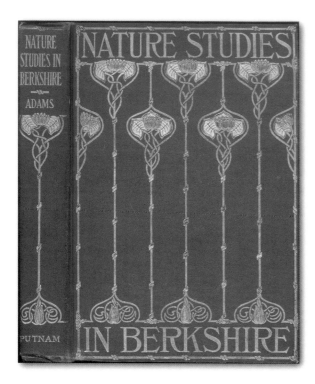

92. Lee Thayer (The Decorative Designers), 1899.
Nature Studies in Berkshire by John Coleman Adams.
Photogravures from original photographs by Arthur
Scott. New York and London: G. P. Putnam's Sons; The
Knickerbocker Press. 25 x 17.2

Green cloth stamped in two-tone (textured) gold repeating
pattern.

93. Lee Thayer (The Decorative Designers), 1898. *The
Song of the Wave* by George Cabot Lodge. New York:
Charles Scribner's Sons. 19.5 x 13

Dark blue cloth stamped in two tone (textured) gold wave.

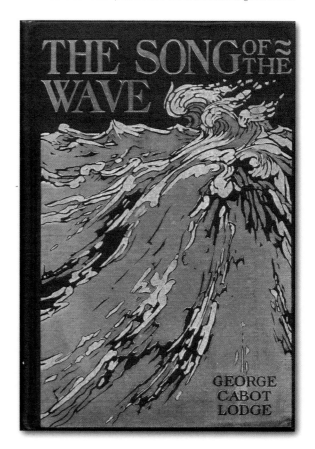

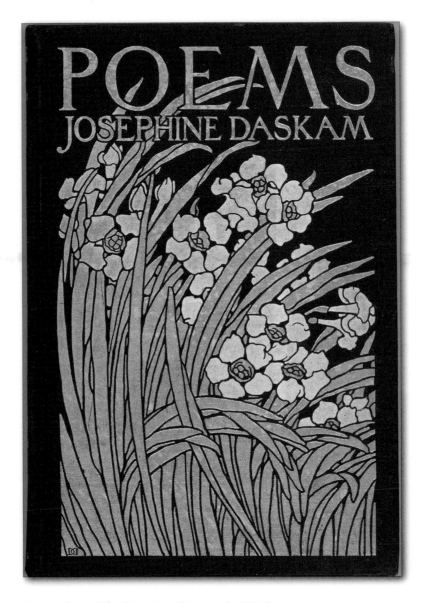

94. Lee Thayer (The Decorative Designers), 1903. *Poems*
by Josephine Daskam. New York: Charles Scribner's Sons.
19.8 x 13.3

Red cloth with textured matte and bright gold stamping of
flowers and leaves.

95. [Unknown], 1886. *All Among the Lighthouses* by Mary Bradford Crowninshield. Illustrations primarily by Lewis Jesse Bridgman. Boston: D. Lothrop Company. 23 x 17

Slate blue cloth stamped with silver, gold, and black lighthouse; silver lettering on cover is part of the design, gold lettering on spine with black, silver, and gold spine illustration.

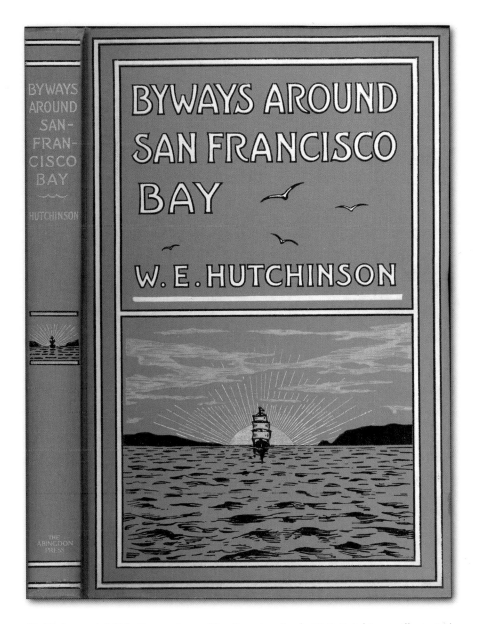

96. [Unknown], 1915. *Byways Around San Francisco Bay* by W. E. Hutchinson. Illustrated by the author. New York and Cincinnati: The Abingdon Press. 20.7 x 14

Sea-green cloth with black, blue, and gold pictorial of a sailing ship silhouetted by the sunset, white title and borders with black outlines.. There is a slight chop on the water, indicating there is plenty of wind. Birds fly above in a separate panel, creating a deep space for the title and integrating the title box with the pictorial image. A line under the author's name holds us to the surface of the cloth. The movement of our attention from material to image to metaphor and back is the genius of this composition. A miniature version of the scene, just slightly different, is on the spine with a gold title.

97. Rockwell Kent, 1924. *Voyaging Southward from the Strait of Magellan* by Rockwell Kent. Illustrated by Rockwell Kent. New York & London: G. P. Putnam's Sons; The Knickerbocker Press. 28.4 x 22.4

Straw color cloth stamped in black with sailboat image, issued in a turquoise paper dust jacket with the same artwork as the cover.

98. [Unknown] 1904. *The Lure O' Gold* by Bailey Millard. Drawings and decorations by Arthur William Brown. New York: Edward J. Clode. 19.8 x 13.2

Blue cloth stamped with white, silhouette of a ship, gold title. In a paper dust jacket with illustrations by Arthur William Brown.

99. [Unsigned, likely Thomas W. Ball], 1901. *Beowulf* by
Samuel Harden Church. Illustrations by A .G. Reinhart.
New York : Frederick A. Stokes Company. 20.3 x 14.2

Blue cloth stamped light blue and two-tone (textured)
gold image of sailing ship.

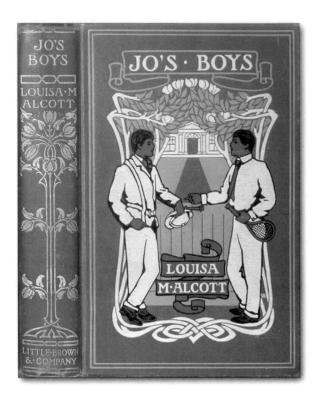

100. Amy M. Sacker, 1906. *Jo's Boys* by Louisa M. Alcott. Illustrated by Ellen Wetherald Ahrens. Boston: Little, Brown and Company. 22 x 14

Olive green cloth stamped in cream, black, and turquoise with a pictorial of two boys, tennis racquet, house, flowering shrubs; spine title and decorations in gold.

101. Bert Cassidy, 1898. *Whether White or Black a Man* by Edith Smith Davis. Illustrated by Bert Cassidy. Chicago, New York, Toronto: Fleming H. Revell Company. 19.1 x 12.8

Beige cloth stamped with black pictorial of a black man on crutches.

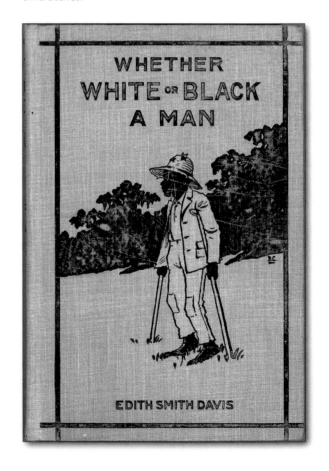

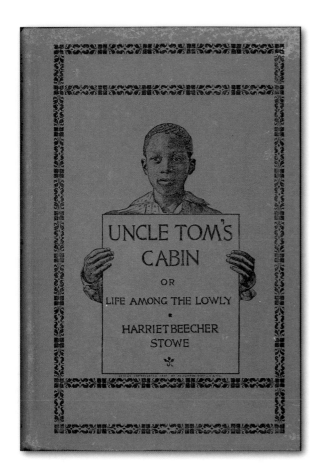

102. and 103. [Unknown] 1892. *Uncle Tom's Cabin* by Harriet Beecher Stowe. Boston and New York: Houghton, Mifflin & Company. Universal Edition. 20.1 x 13

Yellow cloth stamped with picture of a young black man holding a placard with the title, within a decorative border. The Riverside Paper Series of this edition features the photograph that was the basis for the cloth cover; No. 43, extra, February 13, 1892.

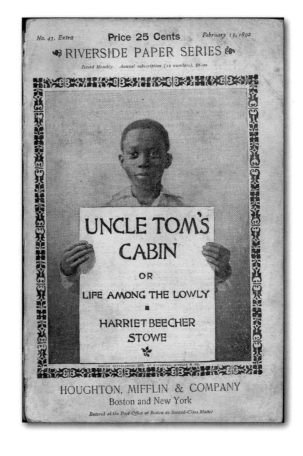

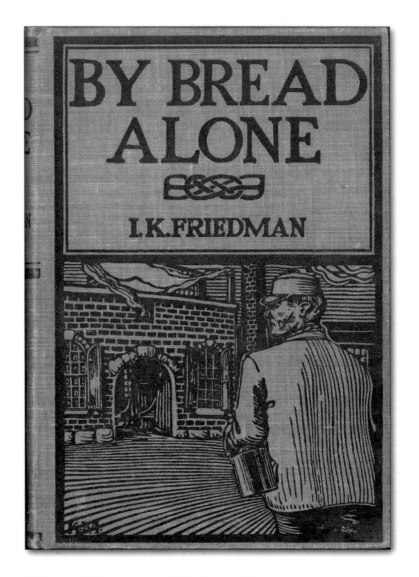

104. [signed K.M., unknown], 1901. *By Bread Alone*
by Isaac K. Friedman. New York: McClure, Phillips &
Co.   18.8 x 13.2

Green cloth stamped in black, pictorial of a man
outside a brick building, black title on cover and spine.

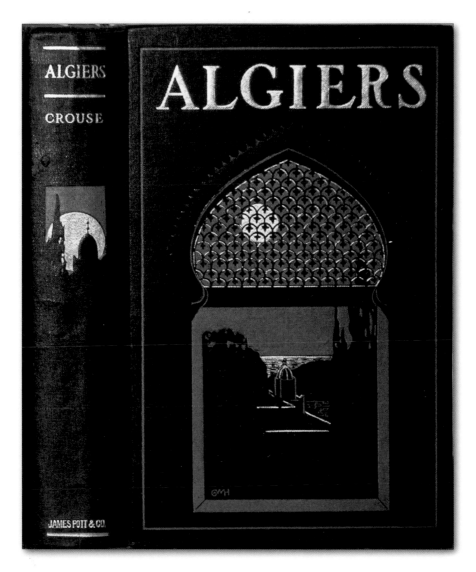

105. George W. Hood, 1906. *Algiers* by M. Elizabeth
Crouse. Illustrated with photographs by Adelaide B.
Hyde. New York: James Pott & Company. 20.7 x 13.8

Blue cloth stamped in light blue, gold and blind of a
view from a hill through a Moorish window looking
down over the roof of a church toward a moonlit sea.

106. Bertram Grosvenor Goodhue, 1900. *The Worshipper of the Image* by Richard Le Gallienne. London and New York: John Lane, The Bodley Head. 19.8 x 13.5

Maroon cloth stamped in gold, stylized symmetrical bee and vine, gold title on cover and spine, related gold design on spine.

107. [Unknown], 1900. Kate Upson Clark. *White Butterflies.* New York: J. F. Taylor and Company. 20 x 13.3

Green cloth stamped in cream and silver (white metal) with field of butterflies, cream and silver sky, silver title.

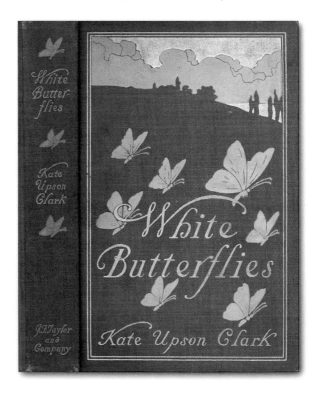

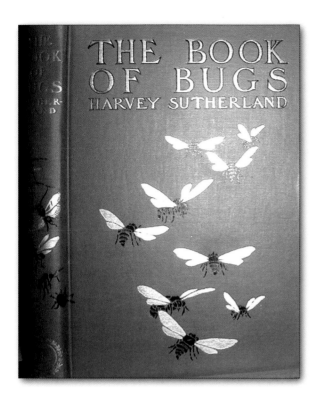

108. [Unknown], 1902. *The Book of Bugs* by Harvey Sutherland. Illustrated with reproductions from U.S. Dept. of Agriculture and other publications. New York and London: Street and Smith. 19.2 x 13.3

Green cloth stamped in black, silver and tan, flying bugs on cover with gold title outlined in black; bugs on spine with gold title.

109. [Unknown], 1910. *Under the Open Sky* by Samuel Christian Schmucker. Illustrated by Katherine Elizabeth Schmucker. Philadelphia and London: J. B. Lippincott Company. 21.3 x 16

Green cloth with yellow, white and black butterflies, white title. Inscribed by the author.

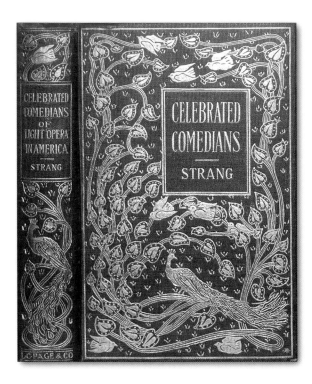

110. Alfred Brennan, 1901. *Celebrated Comedians of Light Opera and Musical Comedy in America* by Lewis C. Strang. Boston: L. C. Page and Company. 17.7 x 11.4

Green cloth stamped with peacock and vine design, series binding with title box.

111. Reginald B. Birch, 1893. *The One I Knew the Best of All* by Frances Hodgson Burnett. Illustrated by Reginald B. Birch. New York: Charles Scribner's Sons 19.2 x 13

Black cloth stamped in two-tone (textured) gold on cover and spine with images of a sailing ship, dolphins, children, dogs, and decorative elements.

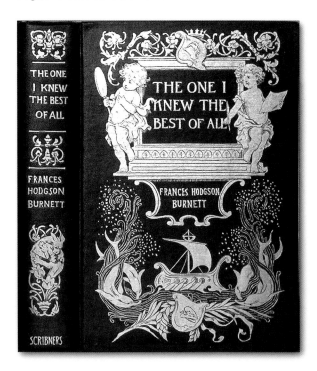

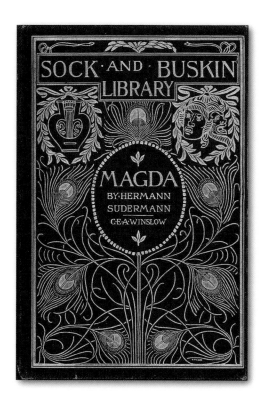

112. Louis John Rhead, 1896. *Magda* by Hermann Sudermann, translated by Charles E. A. Winslow. Boston and New York: Lamson, Wolffe and Company. 17.3 x 11.3

Red cloth with gold design including peacock feathers, theater masks and a lyre, gold title, and "Sock and Buskin Library."

113. Scott Calder, 1898. *The Pleasures of Literature and the Solace of Books* by Joseph Shaylor. Anonymous frontispiece; title page decoration by Scott Calder. New York: Truslove & Comba. 17.3 x 11.2

Red cloth stamped with bright and matte gold pictorial of a woman reading a book.

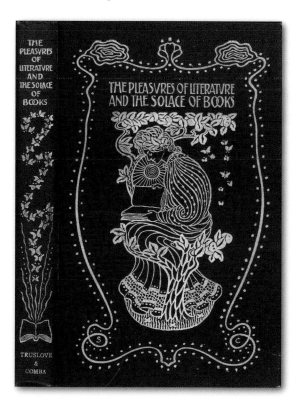

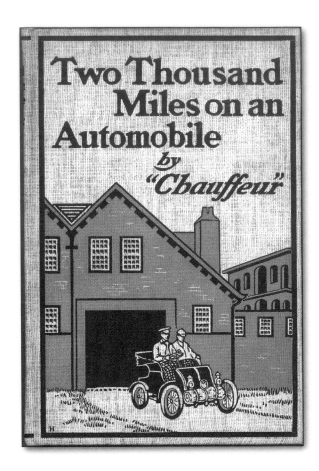

114. Edward Stratton Holloway, 1902. *Two Thousand Miles on an Automobile* by Arthur J. Eddy ("Chauffeur"). Illustrations by Frank Verbeck. Philadelphia and London: J. B. Lippincott Company. 21.4 x 14.3

Beige cloth stamped in dark green and brown with pictorial of two men on an auto driving out of a carriage house..

115. Unknown, possibly The Decorative Designers; lettering style of Henry Thayer, 1905. *The Black Motor Car* by Harris Burland. "Illustrated by Charles Grunwald" is on the title page, but there are no illustrations in this copy. New York: G.W. Dillingham Company, 19 x 12.8

Green cloth with black, gray, and yellow illustration of a motor car running with its headlights on and a cloud of dust behind it. This copy is undated, but has an inscription from 1919.

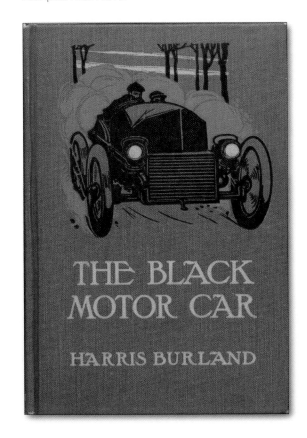

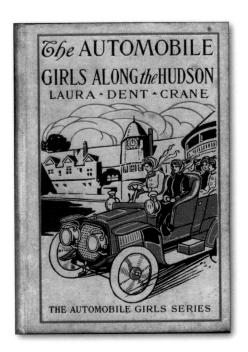

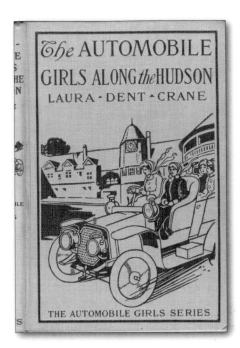

116 (above) and 117 (right). [Unknown], 1910. *The Automobile Girls Along the Hudson* by Laura Dent Crane. Philadelphia: Henry Altemus Company. 19.2 x 13.2

Unattributed cover art (likely by the unidentified illustrator) of five women driving in a motor car stamped on cream cloth in black and red.

117. Dust jacket by Walter Hayn, ca. 1921. *The Automobile Girls Along the Hudson* by Laura Dent Crane. Philadelphia: Henry Altemus Company. 19.2 x 13.2

The later copy (117, above right) uses only the black stamping die from the other edition, here in green on yellow cloth. This edition was published about 1921, based on other titles listed on its dust jacket (right). Although the title page is identical to 116, and the copyright date is the same, it is not the same text, but has been rewritten extensively and shortened from 25 to 20 chapters. The dust jacket (signed Walter Hayn) features a car that is more modern than the one on the cloth cover, as are the clothing and attitude of the girls, projecting a "Roaring 20's" feeling. A great example of how a publisher could adapt a book to a new market in a rapidly changing society.

118. Harry B. Matthews, 1906. *The Man Between* by
Amelia Barr. New York and London: The Authors and
Newspapers Association. 19.5 x 12.9

Black and red~orange spider in web on brown cloth.

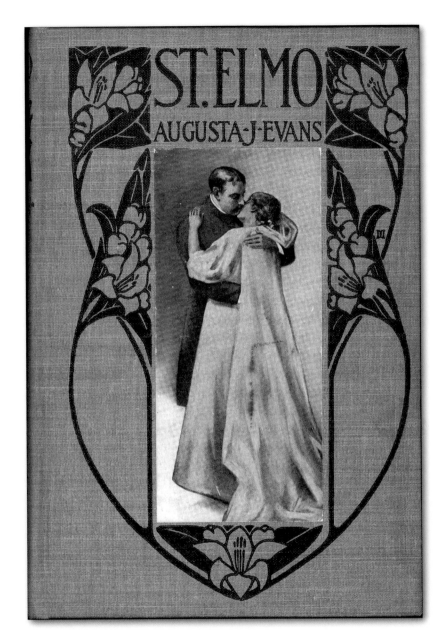

119. The Decorative Designers, after 1896. *St. Elmo* by
Augusta J. Evans. New York: Grosset & Dunlap [n.d., ©1896
Dillingham] 19.2 x 12.8

Gray cloth stamped with brown symmetrical floral border
around printed color image of middle-aged couple kissing.

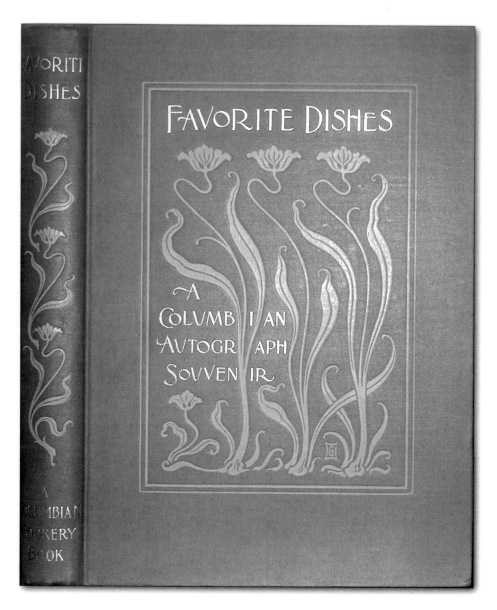

120. Frederick W. Gookin, 1893. *Favorite Dishes; A Columbian Autograph Souvenir* by Carrie V. Shuman. Illustrated by Mary Root-Kern, Mellie Ingels Julian, Louis Braunhold, George Wharton Edwards. Chicago: Carrie V. Shuman. Second Edition. 22.1 x 15.7

Yellow cloth with light gray Art Nouveau flowers and gold title on cover and spine.

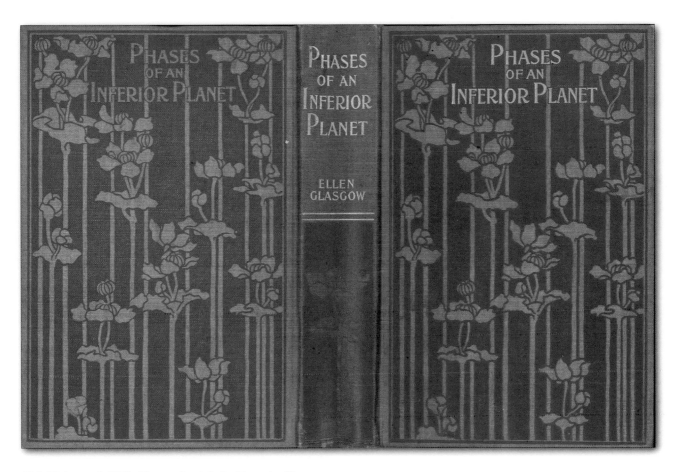

121. [Unknown], 1898. *Phases of an Inferior Planet* by Ellen
Glasgow. New York and London: Harper & Brothers. 19 x 12.7

Beige-tan cloth stamped with green floral design, repeated on
back cover.

122. Evelyn W. Clark, 1901. *The Abandoned Farmer* by Sydney H. Preston. New York: Charles Scribner's Sons. 18 x 12.7

Gray cloth stamped in pink, white, green, and black pictorial of a cottage, black title.

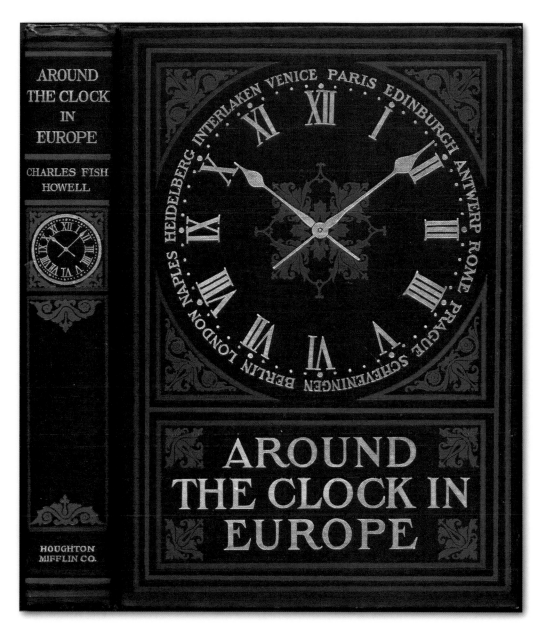

123. [Unknown], 1912. *Around the Clock in Europe* by Charles Fish
Howell. Illustrated by Harold Field Kellogg. Boston and New York:
Houghton, Mifflin and Company; The Riverside Press, Cambridge.
22.2 x 16.2

Midnight green cloth stamped in green, tan, and gold with ornate
clockface, gold title on cover and spine. Inscription from Harold, likely
the illustrator.

124. Maxfield Parrish, 1897. *Bolanyo* by Opie Read. Illustrated by Charles Francis Browne. Chicago: Way and Williams. 17.4 x 11.8

Black, white, and chrome yellow on light tan cloth. Identical design on front and back covers.

125. [Unsigned, possibly F. Berkeley Smith], 1898.
America and the Americans by Price Collier. New York:
Charles Scribner's Sons. Twelfth edition. 18.5 x 12.6

Cream cloth stamped in gray, brown, and black.

126. J. C. Leyendecker, 1907. *The Crimson Conquest* by Charles Bradford Hudson. Frontispiece by J. C. Leyendecker. Chicago: A.C. McClurg & Co. 21.2 x 14.2

Black, gray, orange, and white stamping on red cloth.

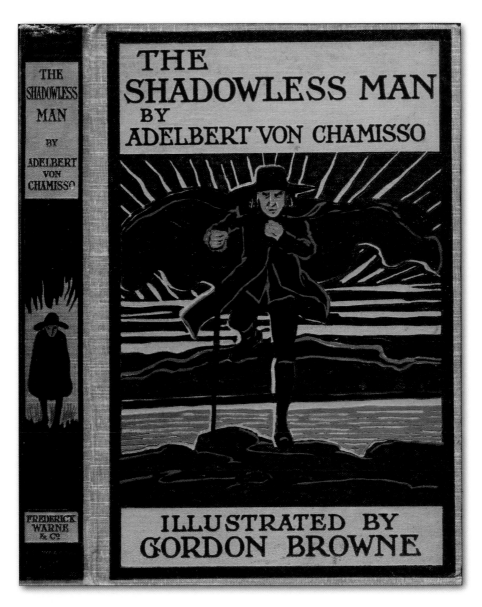

127. [Unknown], 1910. *The Shadowless Man (Peter Schlemihl)* by
Adelbert Von Chamisso. Translated by Sir John Bowring. Illustrated by
Gordon Browne. New York: Frederick Warne & Co. 20.8 x 14

Burgundy, yellow, blue, green, pink, and black on light green cloth.

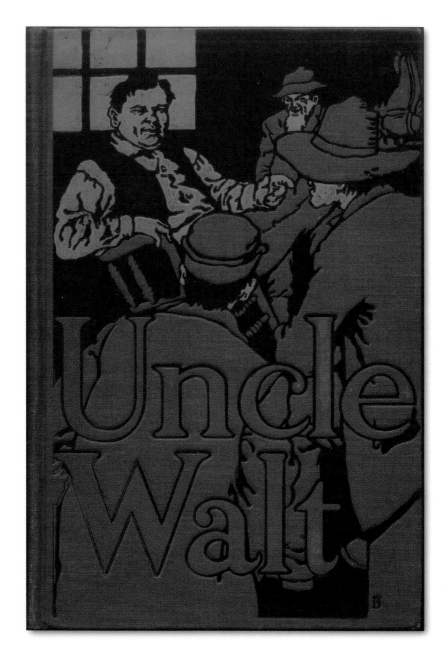

128. Will Bradley, 1910. *Uncle Walt* by Walt Mason.
Chicago: George Matthew Adams. 20.3 x 13.4

Brown cloth stamped in black and tan with orange title.

129. [Unknown], 1913. *Honk and Horace or, Trimming the Tropics* by Emmet F. Harte. Illustrated by F. Fox. Chicago: The Reilly & Britton Co. 18 x 12.3

Midnight blue and orange on blue cloth. The same artwork is on the dust jacket.

130. [Unknown], 1915. *The Crevice* by William J. Burns and Isabel Ostrander. Illustrated by Will Grefé. New York: W. J. Watt & Company. 19.3 x 13

Yellow, dark pink, and black on orange-russet cloth. This design was produced in several color variants.

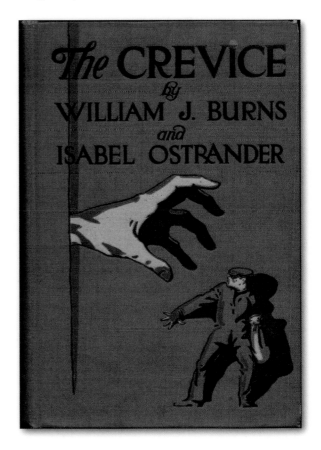

131. John Sloan, 1896. *Cinder-Path Tales* by William Lindsey.
Boston: Copeland and Day. 17.9 x 11.4

Tan cloth with black image of a runner jumping a hurdle.

132. Amy M. Sacker, 1904. *Nathalie's Sister* by Anna Chapin Ray.
Illustrated by Alice Barber Stephens. Boston: Little, Brown and
Company. 18.9 x 13.3

Light gray, light pea green, black, and gold stamping on green cloth.

133. [Signed S, unknown, possibly F. Berkeley Smith], 1899. *In the Klondyke* by Frederick Palmer. New York: Charles Scribner's Sons. 19.2 x 12.6

Brown cloth stamped with pictorial of prospectors hiking over snow-covered mountains, effectively using the cloth color for part of the figures' clothing, with dark gray~blue, black, lighter gray~blue, white, and the title in cloth color outlined in black on a gold rectangle.

134. [Unknown], 1899. *One Summer.* by Blanche Willis Howard. Illustrated by Augustus Hoppin. Boston and New York: Houghton, Mifflin and Company; The Riverside Press, Cambridge. 18 x 11.9

Dark blue cloth stamped in light blue, peach, and cream, creating the effect of a fourth color in the pictorial of a woman on a beach with a parasol by stamping the cream over the dark blue for the dress and over the light blue for the clouds. Gold title on cover and spine.

135. Frank Hazenplug, 1903. *The Country Boy* by Forrest
Crissey. Illustrated by Griselda Marshall McClure. Chicago,
New York, Toronto, London and Edinburgh: Fleming H.
Revell Company. 21.4 x 15.1

Blue, white, olive green and black on yellow cloth. Hazenplug
used a character taken directly from McClure's illustration,
integrating the cover with the content. The depth created
by setting the window into a line drawing pulls us into the
outdoor scene and pushes the boy toward us, apparently in
front of the book's surface. His feet are part of the line drawing,
enhancing the sensation that he is emerging from the book.

136. Rockwell Kent, 1914. *Architec-tonics : The Tales of Tom Thumtack Architect* by Frederick Squires. Illustrated by Rockwell Kent. New York: The William T. Comstock Company. 19 x 13.3

Dark blue cloth stamped in burnt orange and gold with a nude male figure leaping over a golden Earth through a celestial space with stars, the Moon and Saturn. Title in gold on orange border. The border and title are in a format used in eighteenth-century France, while the central allegorical panel is a precursor of Art Deco and Social Realism.

137. [Unknown], 1897. *The Square of Sevens* by E. Irenaeus Stevenson.
New York and Boston: Harper & Brothers. 19.4 x 15.2

Gray cloth stamped with figure and cat in cloth color with white outlines
on gold background at aqua table with playing cards in white with black
and red features, red title. The cat has blue and red eyes, and its head is
repeated on the spine.

138. Lynd Ward, 1929. *Gods' Man: A Novel in Woodcuts* by Lynd
Ward. New York: Jonathan Cape and Harrison Smith. 21.2 x 15

Black printed off-white paper over boards, black cloth spine with
paper label. Same design on back cover.

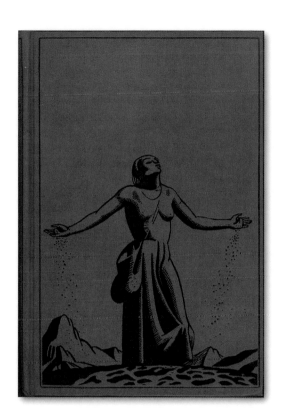

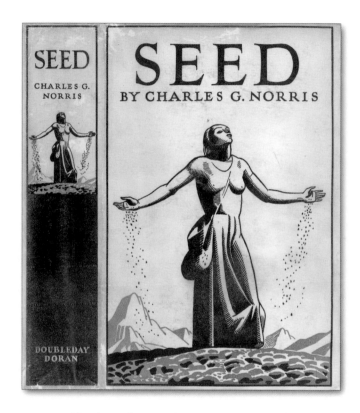

139. Rockwell Kent, 1930. *Seed: A Novel of Birth Control* by Charles G. Norris. Garden City, New York: Doubleday, Doran and Company. 19.9 x 14.2

Brown cloth stamped in black. Title on spine, in black with no image. The dust jacket uses the same image on the front and spine, with titles on both, printed in black and a split-fountain blend from taupe to green. This is a later printing, also 1930. The first edition has the title stamped on the cover, in the same position as on the dust jacket.

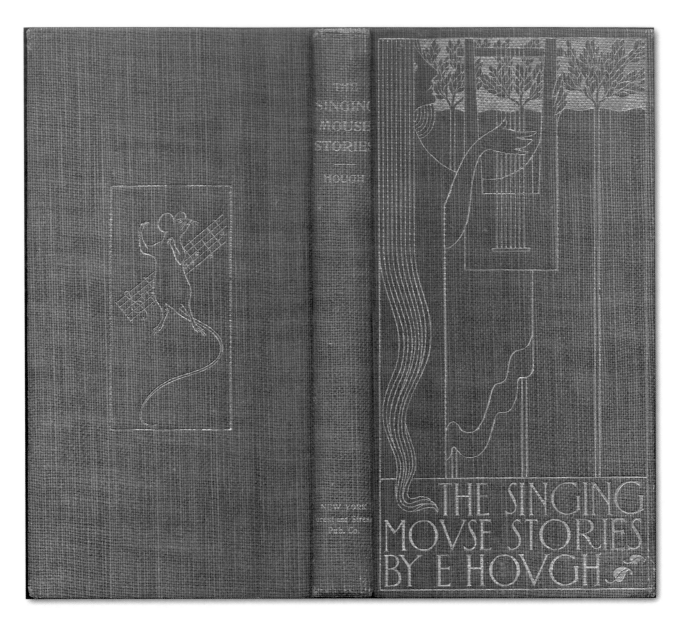

140. Will Bradley, 1895. *The Singing Mouse Stories* by E. [Emerson]
Hough. New York: Forest and Stream Pub. Co. 17.9 x 9.8

Light green buckram stamped in gold. The copy shown is the
second edition, 1896.

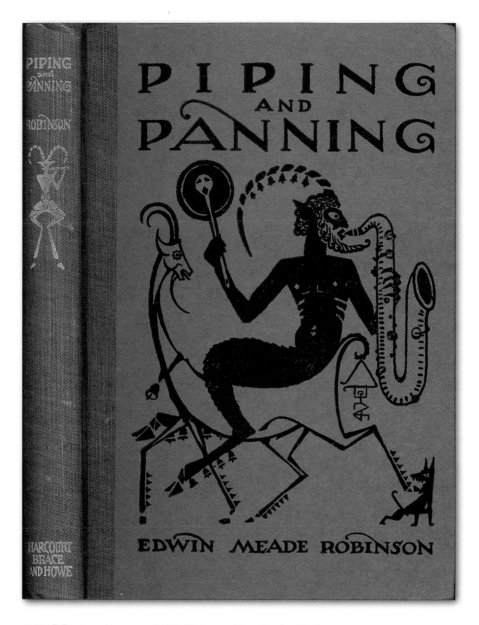

141. C. Bertram Hartman, 1920. *Piping and Panning* by Edwin Meade Robinson. New York: Harcourt, Brace and Howe. 19.3 x 13

Quarter green cloth with gold title and figure on spine, brown paper over boards printed in black with stylized Pan playing a saxophone, riding a goat. A yellow paper dust jacket has the same artwork.

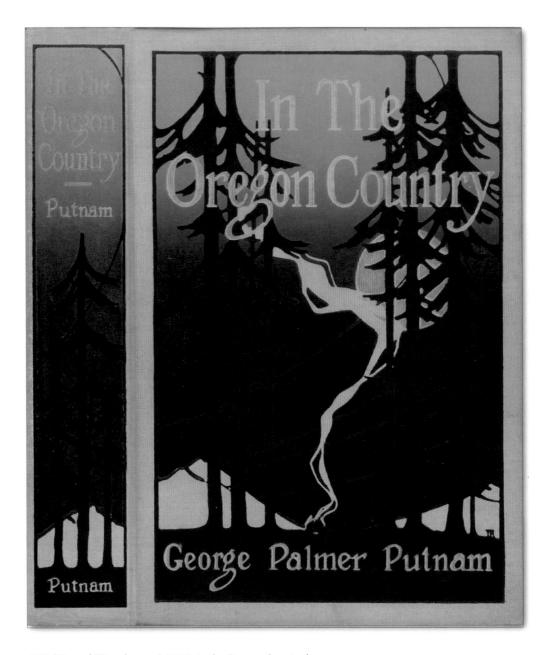

142. [Signed TR, unknown], 1915. *In the Oregon Country* by
George Palmer Putnam. New York and London: G. P. Putnam's
Sons; The Knickerbocker Press. 19.6 x 13.4

Gray vertically ribbed cloth stamped in orange, black, and a
split-fountain blend from light blue to dark blue.

143. [Unsigned, likely The Decorative Designers], 1909. *Northern Lights*
by Gilbert Parker. New York & London: Harper & Brothers. 19.3 x 12.8

Dark green flat-weave cloth. Two split-fountain stampings create this
colorful aurora borealis. The sky blends from blue to turquoise in one
stamping, and the the other mixes green, yellow, and orange in a three-way
split to create the aurora. The final stamping of the title in gold makes the
cover light up.

Artists' Monograms

 Alfred Brennan

 Arthur Covey

 Alberta Hall

 Adrian Iorio

 Alice C. Morse

 Amy Rand

 Amy Richards

 Amy M. Sacker

 Will Bradley

 Bert Cassidy

 Bertram Grosvenor Goodhue

 Blanche McManus Mansfield

 Bertha Stuart

 Thomas Maitland Cleland

 Walter Crane

 Earl Stetson Crawford

 Charles Livingston Bull

 Charles L. Hinton

 "C-box-X" still unidentified

 The Decorative Designers

 Ethel Pearce Carpenter

 Eric Pape

 Evelyn W. Clark

 Charles Buckles Falls

 F. Berkeley Smith

 Florence Lundborg

 Florence Pearl Nosworthy

 Frederick W. Gookin

 Frederic W. Goudy

 George H. Hallowell

 George W. Hood

 Griselda Marshall McClure

 George Wharton Edwards

William Snellng Hadaway

Edward Stratton Holloway

Frank Hazenplug (Hazen)

Harry B. Matthews

H. L. Parkhurst

H. T. Carpenter

H. O. Hofman

Henry Hunt Clark

J. C. Leyendecker

John Rae

John Sloan

Julia Ward Richards

Margaret Armstrong

Mary E. Eaton

Marion L. Peabody

Maud Hunt Squire

Maynard Dixon

Olive Lothrop Grover

Peter Newell

Louis Rhead

Rachel Robinson

Rome K. Richardson

Rudolph Schaeffer

R. Weir Crouch

Sarah Wyman Whitman

Scott Calder

Theodore Brown Hapgood

Thomas Watson Ball

Thomas Buford Meteyard

W. E. B. Starkweather

William James Jordan

Will Jenkins

Walter King Stone

W. W. Denslow

BIBLIOGRAPHY

Allen, Sue, and Charles Gullans. *Decorated Cloth in America*. Los Angeles: University of California, 1994.

Allen, Sue. *Gleaming Gold Shining Silver*. Pamphlet. New Haven: The Beinecke Rare Book & Manuscript Library, Yale University, 2002.

Bambace, Anthony. *Will H. Bradley: His Work*. New Castle, Delaware: Oak Knoll Press, 1995.

Commercial Bookbindings. New York: The Grolier Club, 1894.

Dingman, Larry. *American Decorated Covers 1890-1930*. Catalog. Minneapolis: Dinkytown Antiquarian Books, 2002.

Dubansky, Mindell. *The Proper Decoration of Book Covers: The Life and Work of Alice C. Morse*. New York: The Grolier Club of New York, 2008.

Letters of Richard Watson Gilder. ed. Rosamond Gilder. Boston & New York: Houghton Mifflin Company, The Riverside Press, 1916.

Gullans, Charles. *Monograms of American Designers of Trade Bindings, 1890-1921*. Unpublished photocopy with corrections and additions to 2/14/87.

Gullans, Charles, and **John Espey**. *Margaret Armstrong and American Trade Bindings*. Los Angeles: University of California, 1991.

Gullans, Charles and **John Espey**. *The Decorative Designers 1895-1932*. Los Angeles: University of California Library, 1970.

Haas, Irvin. *Bruce Rogers: A Bibliography*. Mount Vernon, NY: Peter Pauper Press, 1936.

Herman, Linda, and Cynthia Bruns. *TBR: Trade Bindings Research Newsletter*. Fullerton, California: CSUF Library, 1 – 12 (Spring 1991 – March 1994).

Ingersoll, R. Sturgis. *Henry McCarter*. Cambridge: privately printed at The Riverside Press, 1944.

Kramer, Sidney. *A History of Stone & Kimball and Herbert S. Stone & Co.* Chicago: The University of Chicago Press, n.d., ©1940.

Kraus, Joe W. "The Publishing Activities of Way and Williams, Chicago, 1895-98." *The Papers of the Bibliographical Society of America*, v. 70, no. 2 (1976), 221-260.

Kraus, Joe W. *A History of Way and Williams*. Philadelphia: George S. MacManus Co., 1984.

Landon, Richard. *Humane Letters: Bruce Rogers: Designer of Books and Artist*. Toronto: Thomas Fisher Rare Book Library, University of Toronto, 2007.

Matthews, Brander. "Commercial Bookbinding." *The Century Illustrated Monthly Magazine*, Oct. 1894, 842-853.

Minsky, Richard. *American Decorated Publishers' Bindings 1872-1929*. Stockport, NY: Richard Minsky, 2006.

Minsky, Richard. *American Decorated Publishers' Bindings 1872-1929*, Vol. 2. Stockport, NY: Richard Minsky, 2009.

Morris, Ellen K., and **Edward S. Levin**. *The Art of Publishers' Bookbindings 1815-1915*. Los Angeles: William Dailey Rare Books Ltd. 2000.

Oshinsky, Sara J. "Christopher Dresser (1834–1904)." In *Heilbrunn Timeline of Art History*. New York: The Metropolitan Museum of Art, 2000. http://www.metmuseum.org/toah/hd/cdrs/hd_cdrs.htm (Online October 2006)

Only in Cloth. Catalog. Charlottesville, Virginia: Book Arts Press (U. of Virginia), 1998.

Collectible Books: Some New Paths. ed. Jean Peters. New York and London: R. R. Bowker Company, 1979.

Seymour, Terry. *A Guide to Collecting Everyman's Library*. Bloomington, Indiana: AuthorHouse, 2005.

Updike, D. B., J. T. McCutcheon, and **Bruce Rogers.** *The Work of Bruce Rogers*. New York: Oxford University Press, 1939.

Warde, Frederic. *Bruce Rogers Designer of Books*. Cambridge: Harvard University Press, 1925.

Online Resources

The University of Alabama maintains *Publishers' Bindings Online, 1815–1930: The Art of Books.* This collaborative digital resource, organized by project manager Jessica Lacher-Feldman, UA Curator of Rare Books and Special Collections, includes a searchable image database, essays, research tools and links to other online resources: http:bindings.lib.ua.edu.

Richard Minsky's blog: *The Art of American Book Covers*: americanbookcovers.blogspot.com.

Oriental art and ornament references available to the artists

1856 Owen Jones' classic *The Grammar of Ornament* was issued in London by Day & Son and was immensely popular. It was reissued by Day in 1865 and reissued again by Bernard Quaritch in 1868. Jones' sequel *The Grammar of Chinese Ornament* was published in 1867. During this period many magazine articles and books were devoted to Oriental art. Among other texts the artists may have read:

1868 Eastlake, Charles Locke. *Hints on Household Taste in Furniture, Upholstery, and Other Details.* London: Longmans, Green and Co.

1870 Pumpelly, Raphael. *Across America and Asia.* Includes a chapter on Japanese Art by John La Farge. New York: Leypoldt & Holt.

1870 Dresser, Christopher. "Principles of Design" In *The Technical Educator.* London: Cassell, Petter and Calpin. A series of four articles, issued in 1873 as a separate book, *Principles of Decorative Design.*

1874 Dresser, Christopher. *Studies in Design.* London: Cassell, Petter and Calpin.

1876 Jarves, J.J. *A Glimpse at the Art of Japan.* New York: Hurd and Houghton.

1880 Cutler, Thomas. *A Grammar of Japanese Ornament and Design.* London: Batsford.

1882 Audsley, George Ashdown. *The Ornamental Arts of Japan.* 2 vols. London : Sampson, Low, Marston, Searle & Rivington, 1882-84.

1882 Dresser, Christopher. *JAPAN: Its Architecture, Art, and Art Manufactures.* London: Longmans, Green and Co.

1888 Meyer, Franz. *Handbook of Ornament.* New York: Bruno Hessling.

1891 Gonse, Louis. *Japanese Art.* Chicago: Morrill, Higgins & Co.

1897 Strange, Edward F. *Japanese Illustration. A History of the Arts of Wood-Cutting and Colour Printing in Japan.* London: George Bell.

Elihu Vedder's mark
on the back cover of
his autobiography,
The Digressions of V.
Houghton, Mifflin, 1910

About the Author

Richard Minsky is widely acclaimed as a pioneering book artist whose work is collected internationally by major museums and libraries. He is the recipient of numerous awards, including a Pollock-Krasner Foundation grant and the prestigious US/UK Bicentennial Fellowship, awarded by the National Endowment for the Arts and The British Council. In 2010 Yale University, the repository of The Richard Minsky Archive, is presenting an exhibition of fifty years of Minsky's work.

Richard is the Founder of the Center for Book Arts (1974), which has mounted over 200 exhibitions during the past 35 years, and currently offers 100 classes and workshops. He has lectured at many institutions, including Brown University, The London College of Printing, Washington University, and The Wizard Academy.

He has published two limited edition volumes on *American Decorated Publishers' Bindings, 1872-1929*, which are in the collections of The Metropolitan Museum of Art, The Morgan Library, and other great institutions. For more information visit www.minsky.com.

Many of the books shown in this volume are now in the collections of the Hoole Library, University of Alabama, and the Lilly Library at Indiana University, Bloomington.